IMPRINT
CLASSICS

THE

VANISHED

PEOPLE

ION IDRIESS

ET T IMPRINT

Exile Bay

This 2nd edition published as an Imprint Classic ETT Imprint, Exile Bay in 2024.

First published in Australia in 1955 by Angus & Robertson.
First electronic edition by ETT Imprint in 2024.

First published by ETT Imprint in 2020. New edition 2020.

ETT Imprint
PO Box R1906
Royal Exchange NSW 1225
Australia

ISBN   978-1-923205-16-1   (pbk)
ISBN   978-1-923205-17-8   (ebk)

Cover: Remaining seven of the first group of Aboriginal people removed from Queensland, Crystal Palace, London, 1884 (William Robinson for Negretti Zambra).

Designed by Tom Thompson.

Author's Note to his Reader Friends

You and I have been yarning together for quite a long time now. Let's come to a still closer understanding. As you read this book think! Maybe that's asking something, but you're paying good money for it and I'd like you to get your money's worth.

The first few stories call for no effort. You start thinking at the "feather and plug" chapters. You may not agree with my line of reasoning, and may be able to think out a better way of solving the problems mentioned. Thus you will gain more interest from the book. The story of the aboriginal cave paintings and the Vanished People, and speculation on whether the old aboriginal really has a written sign language of his own, will give you plenty of opportunity of exercising thought in a pleasant way. But you must think really hard when you come to the chapter "Facets of the Mind", and the fascinating miracles I feel sure lie deep within each and everyone of us: and you will realize undreamt of possibilities, actually powers, within the you in you. In the "Story of the Swamps" you simply come adventuring with me.

If, when you put the book down, you do not feel you have learnt a lot - and pleasantly, too, then I shall be disappointed.

ION L. IDRIESS
July, 1955·

Who were these Vanished People?

CONTENTS

Mrs Mary Watson.

1

The Mother

By the mouth of the Endeavour River at quiet old Cooktown stands Captain Cook's monument. It was here that the great navigator repaired the staunch little Endeavour after a narrow escape from wreck upon a coral reef. And close by this brave man's monument is a monument to a humble, brave little woman, Mrs Mary Watson.

Mrs Watson was the wife of Captain Watson, seeker after *beche-de-mer*, the sea slug that makes the highly prized soup of the well-to-do Chinese, and of Europeans also. In his lugger Captain Watson sailed from Cooktown with his wife and baby, Ferrier, and native crew, bound for Lizard Island north along the Queensland coast. On this lonely, barren island he landed his stores and rude household goods, then set his crew to work at building a strong hut a few hundred yards back from the beach. The hut was built of stone and mud, cemented by lime prepared from the crushed coral on the beach. A strong door of heavy timber was built and loopholed for gunfire. This rough little home upon a desolate island in a lonely sea was thus rudely though carefully built to resist possible attack, to stand a siege if necessary. As day by day they steadily toiled and the walls of the hut were built up, sweat streamed from the brown bodies of the Malay and Aboriginal seamen-for this was the hottest time of the year: a period of breathless calms with the sea like glass, the harsh granite rocks of the almost woodless island reflecting back fierce heat from the sun.

When in years gone by the little Endeavour was sailing along the Great Barrier Reef Captain Cook had landed here to observe from the little hill, to spy out a passage amongst the treacherous reefs that almost hemmed in the ship. Numerous small lizards had caught his attention, basking amongst the hot rocks, so he had named this barren spot Lizard Island.

Meanwhile, as Captain Watson's hut was being built Mrs Watson's two personal servants, the Chinamen Ah Leong and Ah Sam, were steadily toiling down near the beach at planting a vegetable garden. For Captain Watson's intention was to build a fishing station on Lizard Island, a base to which he could return loaded with *beche-de-mer* from cruises away up along the reefs. Here he would boil and smoke-dry the fish and, when he had secured the few tons necessary for a full cargo, sail back to Cooktown and market. This vegetable garden would be called upon to supply not only Mrs Watson and the two Chinamen minding the island base, but the Captain and all his crew upon the lugger with one-third of their food stuffs. A large patch of that great standby and favourite vegetable, the sweet potato, was planted; taro also, and manioc, banana suckers and papaw, and other tropical vegetables and fruit.

When hut and garden were well under way, Captain Watson built his smoke-drying shed, then set up the boiler in which to boil the *beche-de-mer*. The boiler was merely the half of an iron tank. The ordinary tank used to catch rainwater from the roof of a house is sawn in half, and each half makes a boiler.

Everything finally being shipshape, Captain Watson said goodbye to his wife and baby, gave Ah Sam a smile, and said, "Be sure and look after Missy," got aboard the lugger, and sailed away. He was bound 200 miles farther north to Knight Island, to fish the reefs there for a few weeks. The young wife and the baby, Ah Sam and Ah Leong, watched the lugger slowly fading into the north. Lonely days passed, and all went well. But keen, savage eyes from the distant mainland hills had noted the lugger sailing away; and one night canoes loaded with warriors came silently paddling across the water.

After breakfast the two Chinamen emerged from the hut, strolling down to their work in the garden. Ah Leong went to work at the very end of the garden, Ah Sam commenced work hoeing a patch of long grass much closer to the hut. The warm morning drowsed on, and still Ah Sam worked in his patch of long grass. When he did straighten up and gaze down towards the lower end of the garden he could see no sign of Ah Leong working there. He listened, but all was silent as the grave. Back in the hut, Mrs Watson was bathing the baby.

Uneasily, Ah Sam began to walk down the garden. Presently he paused-he had caught sight of Ah Leong's hat lying amongst the grass. He turned to race back to the hut. A wild yell, flight of spears. Ah Sam threw up his arms and fell but jumped up again, only to fall as another spear hit him. He jumped up again, running for his life, screaming a warning to Missy. She seized a gun and fired from the hut door as Ah Sam came staggering into the hut. She slammed the heavy door, dropped the barricade beam into place as the howling savages came swarming up to the hut. She fired from the loophole, seized another gun and fired again. Ah Sam bleeding from seven spear wounds, began feverishly reloading the guns. Shocked as he was by his frightful wounds, it could only have been the direst terror that urged his feet to carry him to the hut.

Mrs Watson was a good shot. The attackers disappeared, leaping to cover all around the hut.

Urgently the unhappy woman hacked two long spear hafts from Ah Sam's body, hastily bandaged the wounds, glanced at her baby; then, gun in hand, she stood by the loophole again. Silence outside. Just the shimmer of the sea, heat from a cloudless sky.

Away down at the far end of the garden early that morning Ah Leong had been clubbed before he could utter a sound. Had Ah Sam followed him down there instead of pausing to work much nearer the hut both would have been killed and the natives would have crept up, then leapt straight into the open hut.

For several days and nights the nerve-racking siege carried on. Utter silence outside - sleepless suspense in the hut, the badly wounded Chinaman feverishly moaning. Suddenly, the woman went deathly white, her hand to her heart. There was only half a kerosene tin full of water left in the hut! She stared at the row of empty tins. They should always have been kept full. So now, it was only a matter of time.

How stifling it was now in the hut! She stared out through the loophole into blazing sunlight reflecting from a sea of glass. Hot rocks, hot sands, hot air, heat-heat overwhelming. Ah Sam begged to crawl to the swamp that night for water. The woman gazed at him with fear-crazed eyes, and reluctantly shook her head. She knew the natives would be waiting by the well.

The next afternoon, in plain view, the natives launched their canoes and paddled away back towards the mainland. But the woman knew that at nightfall they would turn about and come swiftly paddling back. They would land behind the hill and come creeping down to the water - and wait. They only had to wait!

Her eyes dwelt upon the boiler, the iron tank down by the beach. Two rough paddles were lying beside it. In an instant her mind was made up. It was just a forlorn hope.

That night, they crept from the hut, the mother hugging the sleeping babe, Ah Sam carrying food and what little remained of the water. In noiseless haste under the light of the stars inch by inch they dragged the tank across the beach, launched it, climbed in, silently pushed off. With increasing strength the tide began to float them away. Mrs Watson thrust a paddle against the shallow bottom and pushed desperately to hasten them from land while the stricken Chinaman held the baby and did his agonized best to help balance the tank. Very soon the tide had carried them out into deep water, and she no longer could use the paddle as a pole. The clumsy tank was too wide for the paddles to be used as in a boat; as the tank began to wobble and circle, Ah Sam whispered to her to try to use one paddle only as a scull and rudder. But there was no place upon the iron side where the paddle could be fitted. Mrs Watson pulled off her skirt, ripped it in pieces, and with these rough ropes at last managed to tie the scull over one side of the tank. There was no way of fastening the paddle firmly enough to scull with it, but at least, crouching there under the stars, she could use it as a rudder and thus gain slight speed with the tide while stopping the sickening circling of the clumsy tank.

The rest is sheer, lingering tragedy. Breathless days under a merciless sun, the hot, wobbling tank a suffocating horror, no room even to lie down. Heights of misery as the iron tank slowly cooled off, only to warm again quickly under the newly risen sun. Floating here, Boating there, Boating for terrible miles and miles at the mercy of tides and currents. And drop by drop the last of their water going-gone.

Through it all, every now and then, the dying Chinaman's gasping voice trying to comfort Missy; and through it all she kept a pathetic little diary.

One day, a speck arose from the sea. It was the tip of the tiny peak of Howick Island, a desolate pin-point above the sea. They stared towards it in an anguish of hope-there might be water there! Or might there be natives? The tide carried them not only there, but safely over the coral reef, and they were gently grounded away from the rocks on one of the tiniest beaches in the world.

In terror lest natives come howling out at them, Mrs Watson helped the sorely wounded Ah Sam out of the tank. Gasping in his distress, bravely he staggered away to search for water. Hugging her moaning baby, she watched him weakly disappear amongst the boulders and coarse grass around the side of the barren little hill. The grey granite boulders were shimmering with heat from the sun. The long, silent hours dragged by. Then Ah Sam came creeping back. One glance at his haggard face, and the woman bent over her baby with a moan.

Fearful of natives, they pushed off again with the tide. The pity of it! For there was, and is, water on that barren outcrop. But it was a spring just within the dense mangroves, covered by sea water at high tide. It cannot be seen from the grassy hillslope; but had Ah Sam only been a bushman he would have seen, have heard, all the noisy little birds of the islet that regularly came there to drink and play at the well, to chirp and whistle as they bathed during the heat of the day. I know, for I have watched them for many a weary hour.

When the end was very near, the tide drifted them on to a mudbank of the desolate Turtle Group, mere mangrove islets barely above water at high tide. Here Ah Sam tried for the last time to smile at Missy, then crawled over the mud and away into the mangroves. He wished to spare her seeing him die. Vale to Ah Sam - gentleman.

Mrs Watson's diary had commenced on 2nd October. It ended with these words on the eleventh: "Nearly dead with thirst."

Captain Bremner of the schooner *Kate Kearney* found the pitiful remains long afterwards, the baby clasped in its mother's arms. And the double tragedy of it! For the tank was part filled with fresh water. It had rained heavily just after she perished.

Mary Watson's Diary, State Library of Queensland.

2
Miss Tarzan

IN the wild Kimberley bush, way over the rugged Leopolds, Miss Tarzan's keen eyes see a loaded bee flying heavily. Running swiftly beneath it she follows its flight to its home tree.

In a small, hollow branch far up somewhere there is a wee hole.

That hole is the door that leads inside to the hollow and the wild bees' nest. Miss Tarzan locates it. Gazing up with head slowly moving this way and that she sees far up several "flies" coming to and disappearing into the limb of the tree. With a girlish laugh she points out her discovery to her girl friend whose keen eyes have detected the scratches that betray a possum asleep in a hollow away up another tree.

Miss Tarzan begins to climb. So does Auntie, who has seen, away up in a limb, the fresh marks where strong beaks have chewed the bark from around the mouth of a hollow. Auntie's bushcraft tells her that down in that hollow nestle hungry baby cockatoos awaiting mum and pop to come and feed them; Auntie wants those tender young birds as a tasty morsel for her lunch She climbs on, for she can climb like a monkey.

Meanwhile Miss Tarzan's mate, climbing ever higher up towards the home of her sleeping possum, does a bit of a stretch as she spots an edible mistletoe across on the other branch. That protruding object at her back is the handle of her stone tomahawk with which she can expertly chop out bees' nest, possum, or bird, if she cannot reach her arm down deep enough into a hollow. She climbs on, negotiating a difficult patch where vegetable growths have bulged out the limb of the tree. From the adjoining tree Miss Tarzan pensively watches her mate, with an eye now and then over the forest towards where Auntie by now has almost reached her cockatoos' nest and-lunch. Miss Tarzan climbs on, then pauses once again to gaze out over the great wild bush she loves so much. As her eyes roam out over sweet smelling forest lands and mountain tops and sparkling creek waters, she is alert for possible danger. For where there are wild women there are bound to be wild men, and Miss Tarzan does not wish to be trapped far up in a tree; she prefers the good, friendly earth. More than once she has had to run to escape the greedy clutches of he-men of the wilds.

She climbs on. It is difficult to distinguish her now. If she wished she could in a second make herself invisible by flattening her lithe young body to the limb of the tree, just as a frightened goanna does to protect itself from prying eyes.

But no danger threatens. She reaches her bees' nest. It is only a tiny black hole, probably the size of a pea, far up there in that limb of the tree. Now and then, but constantly throughout the sunny hours, a bee's tiny head and "shoulders", then body, appear crawling out of the hole. He pauses a moment then takes off with outspread wings on his marvellous flight over the bush, seeking nectar of Rowers to bring back to the busy colony working in the hollow limb. As he departs, a tired, heavily laden bee arrives, clings to the edge of the hole, folds his wings, then laboriously scrapes through the hole and climbs down into the hollow with his precious load of honey-laden pollen.

What inborn bushcraft, marvellous eyesight, the wild Australian aboriginal possesses thus to detect the presence of a wild bees' nest! Clinging with one hand, with her legs firmly around the swaying limb, Miss Tarzan lackadaisically pulls her tomahawk from her human-hair belt, and begins chopping. "Chop! Chop! Chop!" the sound rings musically away out over the treetops, over the wide bush.

The startled bees begin hurrying out of the hole, then they swarm out and frantically attack this marauder of their home. But she merely squints at them from her half-closed eyes, blows them back from her nostrils and lips, shakes them from her ears, and keeps on "Chop! Chop!" chopping.

Presently she will have chopped into the hollow so that she can reach in and take out the precious sugar-bag, the honeycomb. Carefully she will place it in the grass-plaited dilly-bag slung around her forehead to hang down her neck. She will slide back down the branch to a comfortable fork in the limb. She will not be able to resist. Leaving a share in the dilly-bag for her girl friend and Auntie, she will lean back against the limb and dreamily eat her own share of the honeyed nectar, high up there where the gentle breeze brings her the perfume of the bush as it comes sighing over the tree-tops.

Happy is Miss Tarzan away up there - her wits about her certainly, but on this perfect day in her beloved bush with not a care in the whole wide world.

3
The Lost Lead

WHAT is that blessed doggedness in human nature that urges men and women to fight on against apparently hopeless odds? We have all read of blind men and women who have grimly battled against their terrible affliction until they could work efficiently at a job and thus recover something from their lives.

Imagine being blind. At night, shut off every light in the house.

Shut your eyes and-keep them shut! Then, from your bed, find your way to the bedroom door. Grope your way down the hall. Find your way through the dining-room, then on into the kitchen. Grope for the kettle, then the tap. Find the matches, and, the box of course being empty, don't swear for that won't light the stove for you. Grope your way back to the cupboard and find the matches there-or wherever they may be. Then find your way back to the stove. Keep your eyes still tightly closed as you turn on the gas. Strike a light. Light the gas and don't blow yourself up-and don't drop the match and set the house afire when it burns your fingers. Put the kettle on. Then grope your way to the cupboard for the tea, milk and sugar. Back to the table for the teapot - if it's there. Listen for the kettle humming, or grope your hand over the spout to feel the steam that tells you it is boiling-but don't grope your fingers into the gas flame. Do the surprising number of jobs necessary to make yourself a simple cup of tea. Then find a chair, and with eyes still closed enjoy your cup that cheers-if you can! Wash up, put the things back in place, and don't spill the milk and mess up the clean floor. Then find your way back to the bedroom, undress yourself, and get into bed. Lie there awhile and think, "and that was only making a cup of tea! What if I had to struggle in such frightful darkness throughout all my life?"

You will feel thankful to turn your light on. For you have suffered a shadowy understanding of what a terrifying thing it is to be blind.

We have all heard of, or read of, unfortunate men and women, maimed for life, or part paralysed, or handicapped in some dreadful way, who have battled doggedly, sometimes for years, until they have been able to accomplish something that makes them feel like human beings again, pulling their weight in the community. Only those who have been able to achieve such recompense know what a desperate, heart-breaking struggle it has been.

That doggedness in human nature, whether possessed by the cripple or the whole man, is one of the greatest forces in the development and progress of humanity. It has saved countless disasters, overcome countless impossibilities, won fortunes and wars and empires. I hope it wins for Bill Heath his Aladdin's Cave of Diamonds!

Bill returned from the 1914-18 war a "hopeless" cripple. His left arm, which he refused to have amputated, was paralysed. Most of the shoulder and upper arm muscles had been blown off. His body smashed by other wounds, weakened by sickness, the doctors declared him a cripple for life.

But the New England mountains were calling, the sighing of the gorges haunted his dreams, the shriek of the mountain parrot as it flashed by his old camp in the ranges tugged at his heart strings. Bill went back to Inverell. Then on to Copeton. Painfully, he built a new camp. Laboriously, he started to build up the health and strength to enable him to burrow deep into the range to find the lost lead of his dreams. This was a fragment of an ancient river-bed whose gravels would surely be loaded with diamonds.

Apart from the problematical finding of the lost lead, this would have been a tremendous task even for a strong, healthy man capable of handling mining tools, of toiling with pick and shovel, hammer and drill, of handling dynamite and gelignite, of working from sunrise to sunset, then trudging back to attend to his own camp duties. Bill Heath had only his own Faith and determination, a broken body, and one arm. With these he had to keep on living and to burrow an unknown distance into a hill through rock.

You probably have read of a lost lead in gold-mining stories.

Never, though, of a lost lead of diamonds. Well, it is the same thing, except that a fortune in gold may lie in the gold lead, untold wealth in a diamond lead. A lead is an ancient river-bed, for thousands of years buried under rock. It is in such leads that alluvial gold and tin, and sometimes wolfram and other minerals, are found; also diamonds, sapphires, and other gems.

Ages ago, numbers of then great mountains of the New England range were active volcanoes, belching fire and ash and white-hot rock far up into the smoking sky, their thundering mouths crimson with the molten lava, rolling down into the valleys white with steam on to rivers that were drowning under the molten flow.

Deep down in the earth's laboratory, where geological conditions were favourable, a furnace would belch out diamonds.

literally then a rain of diamonds would come falling down from the sky, probably into the nearest river or mountain stream. As Time thundered on, the river was drowned under many feet of lava, which gradually hardened into the volcanic rock we call basalt. As Time in its ages drifted by, the volcanoes themselves died. Rocks weathered into sandy powders, rain washed the powder down the mountain sides into the valleys, covering the basalt with the rich soil that began to grow our grand trees and the luscious grasses that have helped to "make" Australia with its wool and beef and crops.

Now, this very thing happened at Copeton, during the making of the world. It rained diamonds from the skies, and the diamonds were washed down into a river. And the lava "swallowed" the river and finally buried it. And ages afterwards men sank shafts through the basalt and found tin and diamonds buried down on the bottom of that same old-time river-bed.

The diamonds found in Australia at Copeton, though small, were exceptionally brilliant as gems, and the best in the world for industrial purposes because of their extreme hardness. When the mines were worked out the miners drifted away, leaving the district to a few score of diehards. And now we come to the lost lead.

There is a lost lead at Copeton, meaning that a portion of that old river-bed has never been found; the lead, rich in diamonds, vanished. This happens with all old river-beds, whether they contain gold, tin, diamonds, sapphires, or no minerals at all. The lead, which is the old bed, is broken in places, sections of it have vanished. This is easy to understand, for the mountain ranges during those thunderous times were riven by titanic forces -volcanic action, earthquakes, landslides, mighty stresses of weight, steam, contraction, water torrents, expansion and other conflicting struggles of the earth.· Portion of a river-bed could suddenly drop down a thousand feet or more and be covered by molten rock, or gradually filled in by sediment; or it could be completely pushed a mile away, or more, by landslides or slipping mountains. Such are the lost leads of the mining world. The miner is working deep down below in the old river-bed when suddenly it vanishes - there lies before him nothing but worthless' rock. The gold, or tin, or diamonds, the old river-bed itself, has "cut out", vanished.

Many attempts have been made to find the lost lead at Copeton.

Hundreds of shafts have been "stabbed" down here and there, tunnels driven into the ranges in a fruitless attempt to cut the lost lead. When Bill Heath, merely a lad, was away at the war, he often dreamed of that lost lead. He was determined that he would find that lost lead if he could, should he live.

At last he returned with broken health and body, a crippled arm; and he has been seeking that lost lead ever since. He has trained himself to swing pick and shovel with one arm, to use hammer and drill and explosives, to do his own trucking and timbering, and all the heavy and skilled work necessary in driving a tunnel into often dangerous ground. The clean, securely timbered tunnel mouth is there under the sweet-smelling grasses where the tunnel goes into the hill, and if you stand and listen there you can hear, far away deep in the blackness, the muffled "Pick! Pick! Thud! Thud!" of the one-armed man's pick. The sweet call of the birds echoes around the tunnel mouth in the bright sunlight.

Bill has now driven that tunnel four hundred feet deep into the hill. Inside it is a maze of small side tunnels and pits where he has dug aside and down as he has come upon traces of some old river-bed. Just a patch of wash-stones and gravel here and there, mute sign that he may be on the right track of the vanished river. Occasionally he finds a small diamond or two - just enough to lure him on-on-on to the lost lead.

Bill calls his claim the "Crown Jewels Claim", and if ever he does find that lost lead then he will unearth Crown Jewels indeed. Good luck to him! For such human perseverance and doggedness against almost overwhelming odds richly deserve success, and Bill has shown what wonderful things the crippled can do to improve body and mind and find contentment. Courage and doggedness can accomplish the apparently impossible.

A strike on the old Palmer River.

4
"Feather and Plug"

Now, while we are among the wind-blown mountain-tops of Inverell and Tingha, Glen Innes and Emmaville, while our subject is insect man boring into frowning mountains in search of treasure, let us watch another interesting thing Man can do against the steel-hard might of Nature.

With only his skill, his puny human strength, the simplest of tools, without any blasting powder, gelignite, dynamite, or explosive whatsoever, he can split in half as clean as a whistle the mightiest granite boulder! Let the boulder weigh a hundred tons, the man only one hundred pounds; let the boulder be tempered down by weather and sun to a huge core of steel-hard rock-it matters not. And then the halves of that boulder can further be split into blocks.

The process is called "feather and plug". I do not know what the taskmasters of Ancient Egypt called it, for surely it was by this process that they split solid rock into the great blocks with which they built their Pyramids; and trimmed the living stone for the mighty monoliths and statues and pillars of temples they erected in city after city. Those were the days when Man believed the Glory of the World was the Land of the Pharaohs.

I know not how this long-dead art came to Australia, whether it was born, or rather re-born, in the minds of her sons during our pioneer age. Presently, we shall try and find out. For curiosity is a priceless aid to humans: it can lead you into great trouble, but it can also lead you to great discoveries.

"Feather and plug" is now practically a lost art. The "feather" is a light thin sheath, the plug is a roundly pointed, tapering finger of tempered steel, similar to an ordinary rounded spike of fairly large size. The only other tool is a hammer.

The process was originally known to only a very few men. It was used fairly often, in the early days before blasting powder, in certain forms of mining, particularly in alluvial mining, where boulders both on the surface and underground so often blocked the way. It was used also in the clearing of watercourses, and for dam-building work. With population and progress bringing blasting powder, gelignite and dynamite, and finally the pneumatic drill, the dead art swiftly died again. There must be very few men indeed still living in Australia who understand it.

One of these, very much alive, is little old Alf Covers. I don't know what age in years Alf is but he can certainly skip over those beloved ranges of his like a young man. Alf was a champion at the "feather and plug" in the days when our grandfathers' beards were black.

Take a look at Alf - posing for his photograph on a granite rock by the old Aboriginal Bora grounds, between Copeton and the Howell. You can only see part of the granite boulder behind Alf: it is as large as a house. You would not think that that little human could split that huge mass of granite in half without the help of explosives; but he could. As he could also this queerly shaped Bora Rock. And the Mushroom Rock. And the little Wedding Cake Rock- which of course would be a shame.

He could take a trip down to Uralla, and split Thunderbolt's Rock.

He wouldn't want to, and wouldn't dare, of course - for what the folk there would do to him would be worse than what the policemen did to the bushranger.

Now, how is little Alf Covers going to split that mighty boulder of ours? Imagine it there on the mountain-side, towering high as a house. From a short distance away Alf looks the size of a mere wallaby as he stands upon it, his keen eyes and mind measuring its position, its "lay", its size, its depth, its granitic hardness. The sun shines on its huge, grey, rounded sides that seem tough almost as steel. That a man without explosives could split this close-grained mass of flint-hard rock appears sheer impossibility. That he could split it so cleanly that its sides will be almost as smooth as a board appears nonsense. Well, we'll sit down under this shady old gum-tree, light the pipe, and watch Alf at work.

Firmly, exactly, tightly, he fastens a tape-measure from the ground up over the rock along its centre length and down again to the earth. He climbs the ladder and walks over the rock to its dead centre, which he has gauged by the tape-measure: and it must be dead centre, for here must be drilled the "key hole". Imagine this particular hole as an electric button.

When all is prepared you press the button and it works. Or imagine it as the cap of a cartridge in a loaded gun. That cap is the key which, when the gun hammer strikes, fires the explosion which forces the missile on its way. If that cap is not in perfect order and perfectly aligned with the cartridge and striking hammer, then it will not explode the charge and cartridge and gun will be useless. Well, the alignment and drilling of this key hole to be bored in the rock centre are as important to this job as the cap is to the cartridge and gun, and as the electric button is to its job.

With exact care, by the tape-measure, with a piece of chalk, Alf marks the position of the key hole. At times, when he has had no chalk, Alf has marked these positions with a piece of charcoal picked up from a burnt-out stump. In perfect line, some six inches apart along the tape line, Alf marks out further bore holes right along the rock and to half-way down each end. Then he folds up the tape line.

Alf now proceeds, with ordinary hammer and drill, to drill the holes; and you can guess how hard this boulder really is as each blow of the hammer sounds sharp and clear through the hush. All that the tempered steel bit can chew out of the rock with each blow is a little powder. Steadily, methodically, Alf toils on. By and by a small round hole has been chewed half an inch deep down into the very centre of the rock, on the very top; but Alf works on until he drills this key hole eighteen inches deep. It must be bored down perfectly straight.

Alf now bores similar but shorter holes all along the line where the marks have been made. Most of these little drill holes will be only six inches deep. Several though, will be nine. One to either side of the key hole, not necessarily the ones immediately beside it. The nine-inch holes are made where Alf judges that a deeper stress must be brought to bear along the line, deep within the rock, according to his estimate of its hardness and shape and depth.

Alf has finished with the hand drills. Now comes the feathering. First, carefully, he cleans out each hole of dust; then picks up a "feather", probably the longest, the feather for the key hole.

The feather is really a tin sheath, made to exactly fit into the bore hole. The plug will in turn fit into this sheath more snugly than a sword into a scabbard. Though this is a "home-made" job against Nature at its roughest, you can guess how delicately attuned each operation must be when the work of that feather is to ensure that the steel plug, which must do closely similar work to that of a wedge, will not unduly bulge the little rounded hole in that steel-hard rock. When pressure is presently applied the feather will slowly give   expand - its presence ensuring that the increasing pressure-expansion - from the plug is perfectly evenly distributed; and also, so it seems to me, passed through the solid rock in perfect line to connect with pressure-expansions spreading out along the line and down in depth from hole to hole.

Well then, Alf gently taps each feather into its hole, to an exact fit. Then he climbs down his little ladder again, and into the lowest hole on one end of the rock carefully and gently hammers the first plug, the first wedge. He hammers only until it just fits tightly. Then carefully he hammers in the next plug, then the one a step higher up, and so on along the crown of the boulder, until he comes to the centre key hole. He does not yet plug this key hole, but climbs down the boulder again and carries his little ladder around to the opposite end of the line. Similarly he starts hammering in the plugs here, one by one tightly fitting them, until once again he is right up top on the crown of the boulder and has come to the key hole again. He does not plug it, but clambers back down to the end of the line to the first plug he had wedged in. And this time he hammers this plug sharply, until it is tight and "solid". A little harder and you would hear the steel plug ring. He stops just short of this. So he treats each plug right up to the key hole, then clambers down again to the opposite end of the line and from the bottom plug similarly hammers in each plug solidly until again he is up top centre at the key hole.

And now, right down through that great rock, and straight along it in dead line, excepting one "break" at the centre, a fierce stress is beginning to gather within that rock. Then Alf picks up the larger key plug; he hammers this down into its dead-centre feather, its sheath, hammers it down tightly, but not *too* tightly.

And now the stress, the gathering splitting power is connected right along the rock in dead line and right down through it, from plug to plug, finishing at the key plug, the control plug, the "trigger".

Again Alf clambers down to the no.1 plug. Sharply, but carefully he hammers this until it just, only just, "rings" - your ear momentarily catches the trilling hum of it. Then similarly with each plug up to the key plug, which again he does not touch, but clambers down to the opposite end of the boulder and hammers his way up as before. And now, if you struck any plug excepting the key plug ever so lightly with the hammer it would distinctly ring. The pressure straight down through there is gathering rapidly now, like mounting steam in an enclosed boiler, except that this great force appears concentrated along that knife-blade, narrow line right along the boulder, exactly the same width right down through it.

Now Alf carefully strikes the key plug. If you held your ear to the rock along the line you would now hear every plug "ring, ring" - ringing as the rapidly growing stress is concentrating right along the line, a long, thin, deep line of some terrific vibratory force.

Alf strikes again on the key plug, and if you were up top there with him you might exclaim, "Hold hard a moment, Alf, while I climb down: it's too far to jump! I sort of feel something might explode!" Yes, it might By apart with a rip tearing "crack!"; but it does not often.

Alf is wary now, all attention. He hammers once again at the key plug, then stares at it as if listening; his hands seem to be feeling the line of rock, perhaps to register some deep inner tension, some faint, quivering vibration. Yes, he is satisfied now, she will soon split. Agile as a wallaby he leaves the danger zone and is down the ladder and on to safe ground.

Ten minutes go by. Nothing happens. Just the sweet call of the birds, a distant report echoing away down along the Gwydir River - maybe a gunshot.

Alf has smoked a pipe. He picks up the billy-can, fills it with water, then climbs right up on top of the boulder again. He empties the water over the key plug. Then climbs down - lively.

Scarcely has he pulled out his pipe again when in death-like silence the mighty boulder has split wide apart, an almost invisible, titanic movement as two great gleaming faces of "live" granite spread apart while we gaze and listen to the tinkle of the plugs and feathers falling sharply down.

Old Battery
Stamper
Bingara,
Geyder
Shire.

5

WE BUILD THE TEMPLE OF JUPITER

AND that is how a mighty rock of extreme hardness can be split clean as a whistle by a man who knows how. If he wished to, Alf could further split those two masses of rock into perfectly shaped blocks of any size.

To split boulders underground is a more complicated proposition, unless the material is moved from all around them. The worker has difficulty in getting a "clear go" at the rock, and the boulder, being part buried, has the benefit of all the resistance of the surrounding earth.

Was this simply efficient "plug and feather" process known to the vanished civilizations of three, four, five and more thousands of years ago? Almost certainly it was. Probably it solves one of the great mysteries of the Pyramids, and of many other mighty buildings that amaze us in the "cradle of the human race". Those mighty blocks of stone could have been quarried by this method. Though the ancients had no steel tools, they eventually had bronze and copper, and later discovered the now lost art of tempering copper. Even the Romans-fine engineers as they were and with far greater knowledge of metal tools, including iron and steel-possibly used the feather and plug method for splitting rock. By what method did they quarry their vast blocks of stone for the Temple of Jupiter, at Baalbek in the Lebanon? There lies the greatest old man block of all time. Though not raised to position, that block has been estimated to weigh 1500 tons. Think of the weight in such a trimmed block of stone! It's not so many years ago that a ship of 1500 tons was no mean vessel. Yet a few of the blocks in that 2000-years-old temple weigh 1000 tons each. Modern engineers still wonder how the Roman engineers first quarried those great stone blocks, then cut those stones, transported them (in this case only a short distance), then lifted them twenty feet above the earth, then swung such gigantic weights into exact position.

Shall we try to puzzle it out? It's fun trying to solve a problem, even if you don't succeed. And in this case we are very ambitious, for we'll try to lift back the veil from the past and see how the Pharaohs built the Pyramids. I really think we have already solved the major part of the question, don't you?, the quarrying and shaping of the huge blocks of stone. Surely this was accomplished by "feather and plug", the method we saw little Alf Covers use. And now for the transport, lifting, then placing in position. Let us "re-build" the Temple of Jupiter first.

Here are the "pieces" to our problem. The superstructure, that is, the great base or foundation upon which the temple was to be built, was erected to a height of twenty feet above ground level. Now, how were the mighty blocks transported from the nearby quarry to the site, how were they then moved into their foundation places, and how finally were others lifted to a height of twenty feet, then placed upon the foundation? Remember, you are handling blocks of stone each from a thousand tons weight downward.

Could this have been done by ramp?

Surely you have seen a simple form of ramp - perhaps by an outback railway siding, or out in the bush, or on a station. A short embankment of earth is held together by logs, sloping up from the ground to its "stage" or platform. The "face" of this stage is straight, and to it the wagon pulls in. Logs or bales of wool are, or were in years gone by, rolled up such a ramp because from that height they can be much more easily loaded into storehouse, or truck, or wagon, as the case may be.

Well, two thousand years or so ago we order our taskmasters at Baalbek to build a ramp up from the quarry to the temple site. And a long, very strong causeway this ramp must necessarily grow to be. Its surface, to carry the great weights and particularly for resistance against leverage, must be as firm as that of our cement roads. Perhaps the surface was faced with flat, movable slabs of stone or cement as the causeway, stage by stage, grew in height.

The battalions of slaves get to work, each under their trained foreman, and quickly the causeway takes shape. No horses to help. No camels either, for history tells us that the Roman Legions first saw camels in Asia Minor in 84 B.C. The ramp, our causeway road, would be built from ground level at the quarry, gently and evenly rising all the way up to the temple site. Then the foundation stones for the base would be dragged up and laid. That huge base would be laid in "floors", floors of blocks of stone, the height of each floor according to the thickness of the blocks. We'll say each floor was five feet high. Well, then, as each floor was laid nicely firm and level, that floor would then be five feet higher than our causeway. So that this leading road would have to be built up again higher, five feet at the temple site, but still gently sloping away back to the quarry. By the time the base was laid the height of the causeway at the temple base would be twenty feet, so that the slope up that haulage way would be considerably steeper than when we started.

The temple base is now laid to a height of twenty feet above the ground, and all is prepared for the transport of the first block of the temple proper. Meanwhile, we've had other gangs of unfortunate slaves dragging along big logs, actually the trunks of trees (they may even have been the famous cedars of Lebanon). Down by the quarry, these smooth, cylindrical logs are placed before the first block. The logs are evenly spaced a few feet apart, then well greased. And now no. I log is jammed against the great square nose of the stone block.
Just a moment for thought-and thought, properly applied, can move mountains.

Those log rollers would have to be solid to carry such a weight and above all to roll under such a weight; so probably they would not be less than two feet in circumference. That would mean very considerable effort to lift the nose of that huge mass of rock up on to the first roller, and our common sense tells us that the engineers would have first used a series of rollers of growing heights, gradually leading up to the first of the main rollers (as though climbing up a gently rising staircase). Perhaps the Roman engineers may have even used metal for the first roller, metal only one inch in diameter; the next roller would be two inches in diameter, the next three, and so on, gradually rising up to two feet diameter logs. Though slow, this method would make the process ever so much easier: for the first lifting of the "nose" of the stone block would be the hardest job of all.

Try to visualize the toil our sweating slaves must do. The greatest of these stone blocks, if figures in an old notebook jotted down during the old war years in Egypt and Palestine are correct, measured sixty feet in length, fourteen feet broad, and eleven feet thick. Just imagine having to lift and push and haul that inert, monstrous weight on a blazing day when the whips were cracking!

Teams of slaves stand out to either side of the nose of the rock, their arms around long, metal-shod poles, really young trees such as the oars the galley slaves broke their backs and hearts over. These are levers, and the lever teams stand ready to force the shod tip of each pole just a little way under the nose of the rock, filling their lungs with air, awaiting the command of the overseer. And key men surely would stand by with crowbars, ready to lever as we would lever a log, or similar weight. Other gangs are fastening block and tackle to the rock, stepping out to either side and ahead now with the ropes, like teams at a tug of war doggedly waiting to take the strain. Surely, too, at this stage of the launching they must have built high above the nose of the rock a strong beam support, a derrick to which was attached other blocks and pulleys holding the nose of the rock. Such teams with downward haul on the ropes exert leverage in helping gradually to raise up the nose. Yet other slaves crouch right down beside the nose, ready to ram in wedges between rock and causeway surface immediately the nose shows sign of lifting a hair's breadth. Others kneel by the first roller, ready to push it under the tip of the nose.

All is ready. At a signal every pulley team bends, takes the strain on the rope. Every lever gang thrusts in and under with lever tips, taking the strain across the shoulder, body bent, chests ready to heave, legs firmly planted. Each taskmaster stands by his gang with threatening whip. The overseers signal to the engineer, a whistle blows. Immediately the gangs surge and strain, ropes tauten like steel hawsers, muscles stand out in bulging knots, a great sigh hisses up as of a monstrous giant's gasping breath, shouts of the taskmasters, then the stinging lash of the whip.

Slowly, painfully slowly moves the great nose, rises a quarter inch to hiss of breath as crowbars jam in under it. Frantically slaves hammer wedges in to take the weight, the whips are cracking now as the hammers clatter on bigger wedges, and she is rising-rising. The whips bite down on the bended backs of slaves whose straining arms are striving to thrust the first little roller under-and at last it is done. A vast sigh arises as, to a signal, two thousand, three, perhaps more agonized backs straighten and lungs gasp in air.

The first little roller is under the nose, that massive nose; it has now been raised one little inch. But that one inch is probably the hardest battle in this titanic struggle.

Think of a long train stationary in a railway station-a terrific weight and mass that is inert. The mightiest job of the engine is first to move it, to force that one first creak of movement, to overcome those hundreds of tons of inertia. Force the first movement, then the rest follows, slowly, then quickly, until "full steam ahead" is reached

The moving of that thousand-ton block presents a practically identical problem. Once the bottom tip of the nose has been lifted up on to the first little roller two things have happened. The pull earthward of gravitation has been partly defeated, and another force can be brought far more into play. That is, the majority of the block and tackle men can now pull forward, for the roller has the rock nose tilted upward. Also, the nose will have a tendency to slide over the greasy roundness of the roller, and the upward movement can be left almost wholly to lever men and to the gangs hauling on that "overhead" block and tackle which directly helps lift the nose.

Do you get the idea? Harness yourself to a log, then try to pull it over the ground. It will be like pulling against the weight of a house. But first lever up the nose of the log, kick a small roller underneath, then pull on the harness and feel how much easier it is. (Unless it be beyond your strength, of course.)

Meanwhile, our Roman engineers peer under the big nose of their block of stone to make sure the rollers just forward are in alignment, and begin the next step of this mighty tug-of-war. This time it is easier. The nose is dragged forward and up to rest on the second roller; it is now farther forward and is also higher above ground, and the dead weight of the complete sixty-foot long block has been somewhat eased. Thus the log climbs up and forward from roller to roller, each time a little higher, each time a fraction more of its bulk and weight upon a roller, each time the pull a little easier, each time a little more advanced, until at last the entire great block is above the ground, and has been dragged up to the big rollers. Once upon these and the going will be much easier. When it is finally dragged up to the site, the engineers manoeuvre it into place, then lift it into position with the aid of sheer-legs, readjustment of block and tackle, leverage, and wedges- and slave labour, of course.

When the job is finished, the temple completed, the ramp is dismantled and the debris carried away. And so we have built the mighty Temple of Jupiter at Baalbek. And all because of watching little old Alf Covers splitting a mighty boulder on a mountainside near Copeton, near Inverell, in Aussieland.

6

WE BUILD THE PYRAMIDS

WELL, you've got the rough idea. Perhaps you think that we've hauled that block of stone, and the many other blocks, all the way up from the quarry and to a height of twenty feet above the earth, perhaps too easily. But now let us consider a number of ways in which the Roman engineers could have much more than trebled the lifting and haulage power they had in block and tackle, greased rollers, leverage, wedges, and slave labour. First, the ramp is a firm, gently inclining upward roadway.

The wider it is built the more power can be developed, for a greater number of teams can work upon it. Reinforcing its walled sides, are firmly bedded upright timbers, probably trunks of trees. Also, at intervals apart, built deep into the causeway itself, there protrude upright similar trunks of trees. These are for the "purchase power" of the blocks and tackles. Such timbers will not be in the way, for the largest block of stone is only from ten to fourteen feet in width. Now, firmly fastened round the length of the stone there could be a huge chain (before the Iron Age bronze; before the Bronze Age - rope). In the links of this, at the nose, are fastened the hooks of the blocks and tackles. Also lengthways, but along the sides, are fastened similar chains. These give links for yet more hooks. So you see that the number of haulage teams that can be brought into power is multiplying. Well, the thickness of some of these blocks is ten feet; some are a few feet less and some a few feet more. This gives room for a dozen long cross chains, fastened at intervals apart around the stone, and thus the haulage teams that can be hooked to the nose of the stone alone has multiplied, with a corresponding increase in haulage power. Now, the larger blocks of stone are sixty feet long. At, say, ten feet apart, long baulks of timber can be immovably chained across the top of the block, each baulk stretching right out to each side of the ramp. At intervals along each baulk; metal or rope loops are fitted, each to hold another hook of a block and tackle.

You see that by now the engineers would have battalions of haulage gangs straining their way up the ramp with tremendously increased power of haulage. Yet another long baulk could be fastened down mid-way across the end of the block, so that haulage teams could exert power not only from end to end of the block, but also all the way down along it.

And the engineers would have known this also: that a block and tackle gives considerable liftage and haulage power, and that there is a very simple system (continuously used in the bush) of fastening one block and tackle to another to increase power, and of fastening these two to a third to secure greater power still. The engineers would certainly have applied many teams of their man power in following this principle. So that now we feel that a thousand tons dead weight may not, after all, be such an utter impossibility to move and transport even a considerable distance.

Now for leverage. This could be applied much more strongly, and in a forward movement also, if applied to the rollers. Probably the engineers used rollers that were the trunks of trees, stretching out from under the block, as the baulks of timber stretch out over the top, from side to side of the causeway that is the ramp. Where each roller would jut out from under the stone block, incisions five or six inches deep, would be cut into the wood. These would be sheathed with metal, "feathered" as Alf Govers feathered his drill holes in the rock, and for a somewhat similar purpose. These slots would be all around the jutting end of the rollers, like the "slots" in the hub of a wheel into which the spokes fit. Only the "spokes" to be used would not fit so tightly, and the slots would be inserted from each end of the rollers right along to the rock itself.

Gangs of men, at each end of each roller, would be standing opposite one another. Those gangs, with their backs to the super-structure, would thrust their crowbar ends into the slots of the rollers and lever hard back, while the gangs opposite would thrust theirs in and lever hard up and forward. Thus each levered roller would slowly turn, helpihg onward the rock that was moving forward by power from the pulley gangs. As the rollers slowly rolled around, so the crowbars would be snatched out then thrust into the slot above and below for new leverage.

If you can picture it all you will see how the great rock could be kept ever slowly moving upward and forward without a pause; for fresh gangs of slaves would be standing by to rush to the places of those exhausted. Added to this, quite possibly the Romans, great seamen, knew the power of the old capstan. (Ask your granddads about "manning the capstan", the crew gang pushing their weight against the capstan poles in winding up the anchor.) If so, they would assuredly have had capstans attached to multiple blocks and tackle and thus added yet again to the power. Those builders of thousands of years ago may have erected their massive stone buildings far more quickly and easily than we have believed.

So, as with Alf Covers splitting that mighty boulder, we see again that simple, natural things, correctly applied, can be made to develop not only great, but vast, power.

As for the various Pyramids, built four and five thousand years ago, the Egyptian engineers mayor may not have known of the simple pulley. They certainly would have known the power of leverage. Their blocks of hewn stone, though nothing like the stones of Jupiter, were mighty for all that. And they built their pyramids to a maximum height of 480 feet, as the Great Pyramid of Cheops, in which, with its five million tons of stone, the great blocks dove-tail perfectly. Many of their so solid buildings are magnificent, even though built five thousand years ago. By the engineer of today, their buildings are admired for their might, solidity, and perfection.

First sight of the mighty temples and buildings at Karnak, Thebes, and Abydos would fairly take your breath away. It's an amazing experience to gaze at the past like that: you wonder and wonder what other things these people knew, things that vanished with their civilization. If those massive monuments could only talk!

I don't know whether there are any new theories as to how the Egyptians raised their great building blocks up to a height of four hundred feet. When I was ruin-prowling in Egypt the most favoured theory was that an army of slaves, carrying sand in reed baskets, built a mountain of sand around the Great Pyramid as it grew higher and higher; and up this sandy mountain the slave teams somehow dragged the building blocks.

But think of the enormous .time involved, the scores of thousands of slaves to be secured and fed, the expense of the armies required to march and capture the heavy replacements, to keep order and police the work. The extra time, work, and expense involved in building such a mountain would be as great as the job itself. To reach a height of six hundred feet and yet be on a slope gradual enough to allow of the haulage of those great blocks, , it would have to be spread round the pyramid for some miles. The piling up of that mountain of sand would have eaten up the labour of countless slaves for a very long time; and then it would all have had to be carried away again.

Don't you think it far more likely that they did as we suggested, dragged the stone up along one great ramp, ever so much longer and higher than the one we used when we built the temple of Jupiter? For our ramp was only twenty feet high at its peak, whereas that for the Great Pyramid of Cheeps would have to be 480 feet. A firm, gently sloping, mighty land bridge, a great work in itself. But far more efficient, quicker and easier than building a mountain of sand, and much quicker and easier to dismantle and carry away.

As to transporting the blocks of stone to their many great works, they would have done this by rollers and haulage gangs from the quarry to the Nile, then down or up river by boat and raft, then by roller and haulage gang again to the site, then up the causeway. Smaller blocks they probably hauled upon low-wheeled trucks.

Well, we've done good work, built the Pyramids, and the Temple of Jupiter. And much more quickly and easily than the poor wretches of slaves toiling under that fierce sun upon those burning desert sands.

What started us on the job? Little old Alf Covers splitting a monstrous rock in Australian mountains without explosives. But where did Alf learn this secret? How is it that an Australian bushman in the year 1955 knows of the methods employed by the people of three thousand or five thousand years ago?

Well, long years ago, Alf came here from Great Britain.

The Phoenicians! Those shrewd, adventurous traders, perhaps the most wonderful sailormen the world has ever known, in their tiny craft sailed strange seas for great distances, reaching lands utterly unknown to the civilizations of their day. The very name of these mysterious trader sailormen brings ghostly memories of Tyre and Sidon, of Troy and Babylon, Nebuchadnezzar and Solomon, of Byblos and Arvad and Carthage and Assyria, of ancient Egypt, and at long last of the growth of tribes of savages that grew into the mighty Roman Empire. Well, one land that the Phoenicians found was called Britain, a land peopled by club carrying savages clothed in bearskin. However, in a wild place since called Cornwall was found an ordinary looking stone we call tin; and in other places a bright green and other coloured stone we call copper. The savages used to paint themselves with the colours they mixed from the bright copper ores.

The Phoenicians soon worked up a trade in tin ores and copper.

For, apart from such isolated civilizations as India and China, that tiny area of the globe that called itself "civilized" had learnt that if you mix tinstone with copperstone in certain proportions, then smelt it, the result is a metal called bronze. This had such valuable properties that it brought about what history calls the Bronze Age. The delight of the Phoenician sailormen-merchants on discovering copper and particularly tin on that savage little British island we can well imagine. And I wonder how many "millions" of the coin of the day they made out of it.

The brave little galleys of these sailormen carried back rich cargoes of copper and tinstone from savage Britain to the "civilizations" of their world. Such and succeeding civilizations took mighty leaps forward the more they learnt of the uses of metals. The Phoenicians, whose ships traded with Syria, Palestine, Egypt and "the world", would have known the principle of the "feather and plug" in the splitting of stone; and they would have been quick to teach it to the Briton barbarians so that they could mine the precious tin and copper ores more efliciently,

The secret, among those conservative British tribes, would have been handed down from father to son. And as time passed and our own civilization gradually dawned a few among the mining men would still have remembered and passed the secret on, even though steel tools, then the discovery of explosives, eventually did away with the need for it.

One of the very few who knew was young Alf Covers who came to a strange, new land, and went to the wild bush. There, now and again in certain districts, at certain works, he finds a job for his secret of the "feather and plug".

So we've not only built pyramids and temples but connected up the far dim past and the ancient world with our own youngest world of all - Australia.

Roper River Police Station. This station was covered in the last flood, part washed away

7

THE SLEEPER IN THE BUSH

A QUIET day at the Roper River Police Station, an outpost of the Northern Territory in the 1930s. Bonnie, Constable Don's dog, is sleeping in the shade. All is silent and peaceful -the peace of the great, lonely Territory. But now Bonnie pricks up keen ears that catch distinctly the sound of hurrying hooves. And presently the rider appears on a tired horse from the timber.

Soon there is movement on the police station. Constable Fred Don appears from his little home and gives short, precise orders. A horse-boy swings into the saddle and goes cantering out into the bush for the horses. Trackers stride out to the rough-built shed for the riding and pack saddles, hobbles and gear. Food, blankets, and supplies for a long patrol are being quickly and efficiently packed.

Bonnie scents action, knows that a patrol is soon to ride out. She leaps up on to the back of a patrol horse, demanding to "ride" with the patrol.

Bonnie is right. Darwin Headquarters has received rumour that months ago a native called Boot, from Brock's Creek district, murdered a native called Frank, somewhere away out in Arnhem Land. The Roper River patrol is to ride out and seek proof that murder has been done, and if so, arrest the murderer. A native named Larry, who alleges that he witnessed the spearing, is to ride with the patrol as guide.

So the patrol rides out.

From a cave overlooking the big Oenpelli lagoon, alive with fish and wildfowl, the Patrol Leader, Fred Don, looks far out over the uninhabited lands. The cave roof is covered, as nearly all the Oenpelli caves are, with the drawings of Stone Age men from Australia's primitive past.

The patrol rides on past queer rock shapes gouged from the living rock by the everlasting hand of Time. And here again there are many paintings, of men and women, animals, serpents, birds and bats, and queer symbolic symbols. But the patrol rides on, having to live in the time of today, not in the time of a long vanished past.

Leaving the country of the East Alligator River behind, day by day steadily they travel on into the wilds of Arnhem Land. Tracks lead them to another cave, the Cave of the Dead, as they seek one of the dead, and one of the living, too. But the sleeper they seek does not lie here. They flash a torch: skulls grin out at them from crevices in the cold, dull rock, dark red skulls, sombre yellow skulls, white skulls, and dead grey skulls pitted with the honeycomb holes of decay by damp and air and the inexorable hand of Time.

For the natives-after weather has bleached to a skeleton their dead, placed upon the branches of a tree - reverently remove the bones, paint them with red and yellow ochre, then place them in the crevices within this cave, their treasure-house of the dead.

Bonnie feels disappointed; she is eager for action. Yet days, weeks go by and her eager nose has not been put on to a job of tracking. Bonnie does not know that in the months gone by the tracks of the killer have long since been washed out by rains and weather; that he may be far, far away. Yet, if he does not know that a patrol is seeking him he may be quite near. Bonnie also does not realize that the patrol seeks the dead, even before the living. For if the patrol does not find Frank, how then can Justice prove that Boot killed him?

So the patrol rides on seeking a killer, and seeking a corpse somewhere within the far-flung wilds of Amhem Land.

The weeks go dreamily by, the patrol seeking news of Killer Boot and of dead man Frank wherever they meet the primitive children of the world. But all look solemn and puzzled. All shake their heads, all know nothing.

The patrol rides patiently on, ever seeking the tracks of Boot, seeking the last resting-place of the dead Frank. Sooner or later they will meet a vengeful man or a frightened woman who, through the ever-present native rivalries, feuds, jealousies and intrigues, will whisper them news.

One quiet, sunlit morning while riding towards Caledon Bay, when all the bush seems drowsing, they ride upon Barachuna and family, with his mate Quepuckie. The natives are surprised and frightened at the sudden appearance of the horses coming nosing through the timber. But the patrol soon makes friends with them and so gains their confidence that Tracker Smiler is able to coax them to sit for their photo. So see Barachuna with all his wives and a few of his babies, and his hunting mate Quepuckie.

And from these shy people the trackers finally coax news. Yes, Boot had speared Frank, so tribesmen had told them, somewhere away out in the bush. But Boot had quietly left their country. One night he had vanished. The tribesmen next morning saw that his tracks headed towards the west.

Cunning Boot. While the patrol rode east seeking him he had passed them well to the south, doubling back towards the west, doubtless to his own tribal country, Brock's Creek. Had he received a whisper from the strange telegraph that often seems to float through the bush, news that a patrol from the Roper River Police Station was riding out after him?

Constable Don now knew that the killer had gone-for the time being. Grimly he smiled. For if it could be proved that he really had killed Frank then a patrol would get him-sooner or later-no matter how far and wide the bush.

Next morning the patrol set out with now but one object in view - to find the Sleeper in the Bush. And Barachuna and his wives and his hunting mate Quepuckie asked to walk with them, to be guides with their local knowledge, to give any help the white man might ask.

Thus they crossed a water-lily-scented billabong, and rode through the wild Caledon Bay country, scene of countless killings and savage forays, of ambush and murder, of women-stealing, and at times of large-scale massacre - from the time, away back, when the big clumsy-looking Malay proas used to comb this coast for *beche-de-mer*, prized sea slug of the sea. The wary, well-armed crews would form strong camps upon the shore, for there they must smoke-dry their beche-de-mer. Countless were the fights between them and the aborigines. Later came the luggers of the Japanese *beche-de-mer* seekers and pearlshell fishers, and fights, murder, and rapine occurred. The hushed bush would awaken at night to piercing screams, animal-like howls of berserk rage, thunder of gun shots, then a flame, quickly growing, illuminating the quiet water, as a lugger burned.

The aborigines, swimming through dark night, tomahawk handles gripped between teeth, clubs in human-hair belts, had swum far out, then under water, suddenly to swarm up the lugger's sides and leap upon the crew with tomahawk and club. Yes, a lurid history has the coast of Arnhem Land from the day of the Malay proas.

Next day all parties concentrated on the camel-track, each man tracking by the side or ahead of another to save time. Had the patrol rode on, seeking a Sleeper in the Bush; and weeks had dreamed by, and still they had not found him. But day by day now they were narrowing down the search, ever seeking that thing somewhere hidden in the depths of this vast bush. Then at last, one cool morning, Bonnie found him.

The Sleeper in the Bush was found just twelve months after the day on which he was speared. They buried the Sleeper in the quietness of the bush.

The long quest ended, the patrol turned their horses back for the Roper. Boot, playing hide-and-seek away to the west, was caught by another patrol. Eventually he was tried at Darwin. It was Judge Wells's first case. This greatly respected judge was to leave his mark on the Territory.

Boot, who was held for eleven months in jail before the case was over, was sentenced only to twelve months, the judge holding that the killing had been done according to the tribal law of feud and vengeance, and was not murder in the native mind.

Maybe the Sleeper in the Bush did not care.

8
THE MYSTERY OF OUR CAVE PAINTINGS

WE have all visited our art galleries, and admired the work of great artists who have portrayed the history of our land. In the galleries of "older" countries, of course, the carvings and paintings go way back through the centuries, offering us glimpses of other ages, and of the pride and fate of empires. These ghostly mirrors of fragments of their past are valued as the greatest of treasures by all nations.

The irresistible urge of Man to tell his story to generations still unborn goes back not only centuries, but thousands of years. As witness the once mighty Egyptians, who have left their story in their monuments, hieroglyphs, carvings, tablets and paintings going back six thousand years and more. From one-time cities, buried under thousands of years of rubble, we are now digging much older stories, left upon baked clay and almost imperishable rock. And strangely human and familiar some of the stories are. Long before Britain's barbarians had learnt to cover themselves with bearskin and paint themselves with woad, prehistoric men and vanished civilizations left fragments of their story to us in carving and picture.

Our own Australian aborigines have done the same, according to their inclination and to their own conception of the message they wished to leave, and their records are drawn with what degree of skill they possessed. This same pictorial urge of mankind has been as strong in our own Stone Age man as in the prehistoric men of Asia and Europe, and the cultured artists of present and of vanished civilizations.

Let us see how far we can support this statement with facts that may, later on, lead us on to some interesting theories. Alas, I can support it very poorly indeed from illustrations, for throughout a wandering life I never carried a camera until later years, not dreaming that I should become a writer. Of the many paintings and drawings I have seen I have put few on record; they were merely a passing curiosity, sometimes a cause of puzzled wonderment. But there is abundant material that has been collected by other observers: in fact aboriginal paintings and carvings have become quite a cult among artistic people and anthropologists.

Through our aboriginal artists of the past, we may sense some surprising things about our quiet old native land: a glimpse as of lightning fading in the far distance of forgotten things; ghosts that bind our land to other lands in the dim spider-web of the past. As all men are different and yet the same the world over, is it possible that the isolated continents were once not isolated, that they were all the same, bound in the one big world? Our world, after all, is merely a speck in the one incomprehensible Universe.

Ride with me into Arnhem Land, then clamber up into a cave overlooking Oenpelli, The walls and roof, as in nearly all the Oenpelli caves, are covered with the drawings of Stone Age men from Australia's past. The photo shows but the merest fraction of the numerous drawings adorning this primitive art gallery. See if you can decipher the drawings, and thus put meaning into what those long vanished artists left for the future to read. If we can prove such scrawls really do contain a meaning, then we have indeed learnt something.

First, you can pick out the coiled serpent, even to its tongue; and the serpent has been a symbol of man from time immemorial. Now what else do you recognize? The goanna? Yes, there are two. And the crayfish is plain to see. Can you pick out the scorpion? And what is that queer looking thing at the top? Is it a honey ant? Or a shellfish? Is that a bird away down in the left-hand corner? See what other things you can recognize. Then see if you can decipher the large drawing to the left.

Now think a moment. Is there anything these drawings tell us, apart from, "I am a snake", "I am a goanna"? Yes, the fact that there then lived animals, birds, fish and reptiles such as live today: just as many paintings and drawings elsewhere show us men and women and canoes and incidents of the hunt and battle, telling us that the everyday interests of these Stone Age men were practically the same as the interests of Stone Age men of other countries.

In another cave there is the painting of a large fish, easily recognizable. Among drawings here and there throughout northern Australia fish have been drawn so skilfully by the artist that bushmen easily recognize them as species of fish that swim in the same waters today.

Now come riding, not with me but with Mounted Constable Don's police patrol, into the wild recesses of Arnhem Land. And in another cave pause and wonder a moment - for some deep mystery begun far back in the womb of time sleeps deathlessly here in this painting, the frontispiece.

A man may be pardoned if he muses that perhaps the secret brooding here fades back even farther than the misty Dreamtime of the aborigines, the Dreamtime that signifies to them the very beginning of things. For the aborigines themselves do not know even in legend the vanished people whose once-living hands painted these queer figures. Even the wise men among the aborigines regard these paintings with awe, shaking their heads and gazing silently down when questioned about them.

What people really did paint these strange figures, figures with queer headdresses, some with haloes, some like the rays of the sun, all without a mouth, some clothed in skirts, others almost like mummies? Some of these paintings are vividly coloured.

These peculiar paintings have been found only in caves in the isolated Kimberley country, far to the west in Western Australia's rugged north, and here in a very few secluded places in Arnhem Land. I have only seen them in the Kimberleys myself. The photo is not of the best, unfortunately; it was taken in bad light by the small camera carried by Don's wandering police patrol. Use your magnifying glass and see if you can puzzle out any meaning in these queer figures, the originals of which may have been painted in that dim age when Australia was a land of mighty mountains, rivers and forests, over which roamed the dinosaur, the diprotodon, the sabre-toothed tiger, the giant crocodile, the giant kangaroo and wombat, and other prehistoric monsters.

The first of these strange paintings was discovered away back in 1838 by a remarkable man, Sir George Grey. Of indomitable spirit, he had a life crammed with adventure. Much more useful than that, he was a keen and brainy worker and left his mark in the foundation of South Australia, New Zealand and the Cape Colony. His finding of the cave paintings along the most inaccessible coastline of Australia in those early years was but the merest episode in an extraordinarily active and useful life. Landing from an exploration ship in Brunswick Bay with Lieutenant Lushington, he trudged inland and discovered the Glenelg River, and in a cave the first of these paintings. His excellent description has kept the world guessing as to the origin of these paintings right up to this day. He stayed but a very short time in the vicinity, leaving that wild area to the aborigines. Only within recent years, as a dozen or so settlers have pushed out into that maze of rugged little ranges, have more such cave paintings been found.

However, the paintings are to be found in a considerably larger area of country, and are much more numerous, than is generally supposed, even though they are not of such vivid colourings as in the vicinity of the Glenelg and Prince Regent. I have seen quite a number of them when merely riding with a Kimberley police patrol, from south to north, under sheltering ledges upon the rock faces, right from the Isdell Gorge to the Prince Regent. Mostly one sees rows of figures, some only head and shoulders, others full size; and generally, beside them, the skulls and bones of the dead. Such bones are often painted, particularly in red ochre: this custom goes back to farthest antiquity. We know that back to five thousand years ago red was believed to be a magical colour, and red ochre was therefore used by various ancient races for painting the bones of their dead. It was thus in Byblos with which town the Egyptians traded five thousand years ago, and the Phoenicians even before that. It is strange that a custom of an ancient civilization in a far distant land should also have been a custom of our own aborigines from time unknown.

How did that custom come here? And how is it that it held the same significance to Australian aborigines as it did to the citizens of the most ancient, still living town in the world?

The colours used in these Kimberley cave paintings are red, white, yellow and black. Most of the figures are fully clothed, some with that queer-looking "halo" headdress, if such it be, others with a headdress that resembles the rays of a rising sun; some with both. Strangely, none of the figures are painted with a mouth. Some have a queer looking dress, others have part dress, part pants; an occasional one seems to be in the wrappings of a mummy, except that face and hands are uncovered. The main part of them all appears to be the head, the neck to just below the shoulders, with large eyes and nose, so very different to the usual aboriginal drawings. Below the neck of most hangs what is apparently a large ornament, oblong-shaped. Possibly the original was carved from pearl-shell. Among some of these paintings, though not all, are drawings of the giant serpent of legend, going back to the creation of things.

One ledge painting intrigued me a lot, for there, from the mouths of two such giant serpents protruded outstretched legs, feet, arms and hands of human beings. If those two serpents weren't represented as gobbling up those human beings, then I'm just plain stupid. Although on the same ledge are ordinary sized paintings of humans, the legs and hands outstretched from the serpents' mouths are those of fairies. But then, as we'll learn later, the aboriginal artist seldom pays attention to proportion as we do. His main object is to identify to his tribesmen what he is endeavouring to represent. And those tiny, fairy-like arms and legs, to those who understand, are those of full-grown men and women being gobbled up.

Did some unknown, long extinct Australian race draw these drawings in the first place? Or did the succeeding aboriginal tribes copy the idea of a tiny drawing to represent a subject immeasurably larger? If such paintings were first done by shipwrecked sailors, as one theory holds, then such a "civilized" artist surely would have drawn more in proportion.

On some ledges also are numerous imprints of the "shadow hands", which we'll inquire into later. Of other drawings I could not make either head or tail, while the Patrol Officer just shrugged.

"What use to ask?" He smiled. "They'll never tell you-about these! Even if they know, which I doubt."

Trudging along with us, generally eager to answer questions and even volunteer information, were a medley of prisoners, witnesses, and sick people, the latter following us even for hundreds of miles in the desperate hope of being cured when we should return to the "White Man Camp Derby", and our trackers, two of them especially trusted and intelligent. (Old Larry, the "boss" tracker, already decorated, has since been taken all the way south to be honoured by meeting the Queen.)

To all my inquiries about the paintings, and my promises of rich rewards in tobacco, pipes, and clothes, all hands were simply mute, and obviously uneasy. Old Larry, anxious to be pushing on, would expressively answer, "No man can tell him that one! No man know!" Which I knew to be a white lie on Old Larry's part, for, although the aborigines may not know the origin of these paintings, there is certainly something deeply sacred or secret about them.

Bonnie finds
the "Sleeper
in the Bush".

9

THE MYSTERY OF THE KIMBERLEYS

WHO were the originators of these primitive paintings, if they were not done by aboriginal ancestors of the present race? There are several theories. One was that the originals were done by an unknown people who lived in those very few localities before the ancestors of the present aborigines arrived. If so, that mysterious race has left no other trace or memory than those queer paintings.

Another theory is that the paintings were the work of Malay seamen of more than a century ago, sailing our coastal waters in search of pearl-shell and *beche-de-mer*. But surely the aborigines would know if such work was done by such recent and such hostile visitors! And the aborigines would not accept as sacred the work of men they regarded as piratical invaders.

As, against this theory also, the Kimberley portion of the coastline is the most inaccessible in Australia, walled by cliffs, tortured by outrageous tides. And, though rich in pearl-shell, it is poor in comparison with the north and north-eastern waters in *beche-de-mer*. Much easier of access to what is now Indonesia lies the three thousand miles of mostly low-lying coastline of the Territory and the north-where, in Arnhem Land, Constable Don took that photo of the "Hooded Man", the only such painting that I've heard of there, by the way. Along that coastline in the shallows, from time immemorial there have been vast beds of *beche-de-mer*, and pearl-shell, too, though in deeper waters.

As to pearl-shell, it has been fished for centuries in Indonesian waters, such as near the Am Islands. It is much easier fishing there, than making that long, dangerous voyage, sailing and returning once a year with the change of the seasonal winds. As to *beche-de-mer*, although its seekers claimed a few isolated camps ashore where they gathered in force to smoke-dry their catch, they never ventured inland. Vastly greater numbers of hostile natives would have barred their way.

How then could the Malays have left such paintings deep inland and far to the nor'-west, within the caves and gorges of possibly the roughest and certainly most inaccessible area of Australia. They simply did not. Their whole interest was self-protection, the necessity to work hard and long, to smoke-dry their catch as quickly as possible, to get it aboard the proas, to continue fishing or to sail back home.

They would have had neither time nor inclination to paint at some coastal camp where the local aborigines would have copied the designs and "traded" them to other tribes hundreds of miles away. Though the aborigines themselves swear that the paintings were done by another race far away back "near the Dreamtime", that race could not have been the Malays. And whether any of the numerous Malayan races have painted such drawings in their homelands I've never learnt.

Another theory, and now the generally accepted one, is that the originals were drawn by ship-wrecked white sailors, those venturesome mariners of the old Dutch, Portuguese, and Spanish fleets. If so, they must have been good men to have survived long enough under such harsh and strange conditions, to have survived the certain attacks of far superior numbers of hostile natives, and at the same time to have learnt the whereabouts of the necessary ochres and turned them into pigments. And if a Robinson Crusoe among such castaways *did* survive why did he leave such strange paintings? Why did the artist castaways not leave their own names, the names of their ships, as we surely would have done? Why did they not paint a ship, or a house of their own land, or the thousand simple things they must have been pining to see again? Such must have been in their hearts, and by such simple things rescuers could have identified them. But they left not even the sketch of an anchor, or a date, or a sketch of a sweetheart. We have only these "one sort" queer drawings, which even now we are unable to decipher. Drawings without a mouth.

As to wrecks to provide the castaways: The majority of wrecks throughout the centuries were never recorded; there were merely ships that vanished, brave little vessels sailing the unknown, Portuguese, Dutch, or Spanish. A few coins of the early fifteenth century have been found on the Western Australian coast. Still, we can find known instances in the seventeenth century. From the Royal Archives at The Hague, there is the wreck of the *e ergulde raeck* (*Golden ragon*) in April 1656. Seventy-five of the 193 people reached shore; of these, seven sailed in a ship's boat to Batavia for help; of the 68 survivors ashore none was ever heard of again. These unfortunates could not have started the cave paintings, for their wreck was a thousand miles and more south of the Kimberleys; and any record they would have left would have been something to help their hoped-for rescuers from Batavia to find or at least identify them.

According to the old archives the *Golden ragon* had aboard 78,600 guilders packed snugly in eight boxes. So there lies to this day a handy treasure trove for the modern diver very close to our Western Australian coast. If you happen to be a venturesome frogman with a kink for seeking sunken treasure, then read *Sailormen s Ghosts.* Malcolm Uren, an authority on old Western Australian coastal history, has dealt far more exhaustively with such old wrecks than can be done here. And don't blame me if you don't find the treasure.

Another noted wreck was that of the *atavia,* Pelsart's ship that struck a reef on the Houtman Abrolhos in 1629. This was the scene of a terrible massacre of men, women and children by the mutineers. But here again the scene is a thousand miles south of the Kimberleys; and the survivors, fighting their long, pitiless fight on these desolate islands twenty miles and more from the coast, would not have had inclination, time, or opportunity to paint a model for the far-distant cave paintings. (Most of the. treasure in this tragic wreck was recovered. But one case containing eight thousand Rix guilders still lies there, according to old records. If you're interested you'll find it very fully recorded in *Sailormen s Ghosts.*)

There are a very few recorded instances of a boatload of sailors going ashore, wandering into the bush, and never returning. It is almost impossible to believe that any of these desperate unfortunates could have been responsible for the cave paintings. Thus we can stretch back for three hundred years and prove that a few, but very few, castaways reached the Western Australian coast. There have been many wrecks since, but nearly all far to the south. Doubtless a few castaways from these reached the coast - to vanish.

I think we've given the shipwrecked mariner theory a fair go. But here's one more little mystery. In 1916 H.M.A.S. *Encounter,* on patrol duty, put into Napier Broome Bay. This bay is quite close to Brunswick Bay, where Sir George Grey started inland, and quite near the Glenelg River where he found the first cave paintings. An old friend of mine, Com. Stephens, and Surgeon-Lieutenant Roberts went ashore to stretch their legs on a tiny island, and received the thrill of their eventful lives to find the verdigris-covered muzzles of two small carronades sticking up out of the sand.

Aboard the *Encounter* there was a rush of volunteers to dig up the carronades. Armed with picks and shovels, excited with visions of chests of doubloons and pieces of eight, glittering jewels and millions in golden ducats, the Aussie jack-tars set to work with a will. But alas, no treasure was dug out, though the sweat the party lost swelled the tide-so they swear.

When cleaned, the carronades were found to bear the sign of the Portuguese Crown and Rose. Rubbings of these were eventually mailed to Portugal, and the reply received was that the carronades were cast during the late fifteenth or early sixteenth century. The carronades are now mounted by the Royal Yacht Club, Sydney. So right in the very locality of the first discovered cave paintings is evidence of mishap or shipwreck going back three hundred and fifty years.

Though the crew of that unknown vessel, in sheltered waters and close to the shore, may have rowed ashore well armed and amply provisioned to live their hapless lives away, none may have gone ashore at all. The islet may well have been made a base, the carronades landed for defence while the vessel was being repaired. Then she sailed away. But why were two valuable carronades left behind? The little ship may have been forced to leave in a hurry. She may have been overwhelmed, and burned, and every man slaughtered. For the aborigines there were numerous; they are great water men too, whether upon or under water. In the time necessary to repair a vessel they could well have lost their first awe of the strange white visitants. If they swarmed aboard in the night, it would have been all over within moments, for the natives would suddenly have appeared, bounding all over the vessel as if they were devils shot up from the very depths. Like this they have overwhelmed Malay proas and armed Japanese fishing vessels in recent years.

I don't believe that shipwrecked sailors painted these strange figures. Would they have drawn figures without mouths? Wouldn't they also have drawn other things: the sign of the Cross if they were Christians, some religious or national symbol? Or a carronade, a cutlass, a pike, their own ship's figurehead? Wouldn't they have drawn a girl, a mermaid?

Let us make a guess ourselves! What if the original drawings were the work of some weather-blown Phoenician or Egyptian galley seamen, of three, even five thousand years ago? The mysterious Phoenicians in particular were great seamen. The aborigines would have looked upon such visitants as white spirits come down from the skies, and thus the strangers could have survived. Those strange paintings may well represent some religious Phoenician belief.

We have some faint, elusive basis for our wild guess anyway. For here and there, you see ornament, or learn of rite, or notice some particular "layout" in stonework upon sacred grounds, or some particular sign or carving, that vaguely brings memory back to something seen in the Egyptian museums. There is also a "ghostly" interweaving of mystic beliefs from the vanished civilizations of other lands. The Sacred Trees, for instance, and the belief in divinities residing there, so strong a belief among all Australian aborigines; and the greatly revered Sacred Stones. Many such stones are preserved today in the big temple of Byblos, and that town traded with Phoenicia and Egypt five thousand years ago. Does it not seem strange to you that a number of the strongest mystical beliefs of ancient civilization should also be among the strongest mystical beliefs of our own Australian aborigines! Where did our isolated Stone Age men acquire such beliefs? Did they bring them with them to this land?

I've mentioned the painting of the bones of the dead with the symbolic red of red ochre. The same "magical" colour was used, the same symbolism was practised, by the ancients of Asia Minor. Then again, in our Torres Strait islands, far nor'-east of the Kimberleys, the priests of the islanders in crude fashion used to mummify their dead.

But this is all guess work. We do not know what people painted the first of these paintings, that have since been kept reverently "in order" by our Stone Age aborigines. Before we leave the locality of those mystery paintings, I must mention another drawing entirely different in type which I believe to be almost as intriguing as the "mouthless men".

This drawing is not mine; it was drawn from the original by Joseph Bradshaw, M.R.G.S.A., and reproduced in the *Transactions of the Royal Geographical Society of ustralasia*. He carried out a venturesome trip over the King Leopold Ranges seeking land towards the Prince Regent River, and the short account of his journey was read before the Society in 1891. Here is his own description of these particular cave paintings:

e followed the course of this rince Regent River upwards for five days, and found that it emerged in an immense volume from a gorge in some inaccessible ranges. e saw numerous caves and recesses in the rocks, the walls of which were adorned with native paintings, coloured in red, black, brown, yellow, white, and a pale blue. Some of the human figures were life si e, the bodies and limbs were attenuated, and represented as having numerous tassel shaped adornments appended to the hair, neck, waist, arms, and legs but the most remarkable fact in connection with these drawings is that wherever a profile face is shown the features are of a most pronounced aquiline type, quite different from those of any native we encountered. Indeed, looking at some of the groups, one might almost think himself viewing the painted walls of an Egyptian temple. These sketches seemed to be of great age, but over the surface of some of them were drawn in fresher colours smaller and more recent scenes, and rude forms of animals, such as the kangaroo, wallaby, porcupine, crocodile, etc. In one or two places we. noticed alphabetical characters, somewhat similar to those seen by Sir George Grey in nearly the same latitude, but many miles westward, on the Glenelg Rover.

There is Bradshaw's account. The country was just as wild. when I rode through there twenty years ago, and I saw no white man, only natives, along that rock-walled, beautifully picturesque river. To the best of my knowledge it is just as wild today. A well-equipped trip through that maze of gorges and cliffs and mountain torrents might discover surprising things.

What takes your eye with this sketch? (see page 48). Firstly, perhaps, the fact that the drawings are much truer to life than the usual crude aboriginal drawings; secondly, the European style of features; thirdly, the queer headdresses. The queer way, too, of wearing an apparent belt, with its tassel-like ornaments; and possibly the delicate hands and fingers; and those figures on top that almost look like a form of writing. Paintings such as this and those of the mouthless men, though so utterly different, may be in some manner connected. Let us see if we can read anything into this drawing. First, we all recognize the kangaroo. Then there is the serpent, obviously the Great Serpent of aboriginal mythology: many races all over the world had a Sacred Serpent in their mythology.

It is very difficult to believe that ancestors of the present race of aborigines drew those Europeanized, Semitic, Arabic countenances. The hat, if so it be, on the placid-looking bearded man, faintly reminds me of quaint headgear glimpsed on similar looking persons strolling through bazaars in the Middle East; and I remember in a Middle East museum an almost exactly similar drawing of a headdress done in stone, a headdress as worn by the priests of the ancient city of Palmyra. The figure with the legs is apparently a lady with "hair-do" such as I've never seen worn in half a lifetime of wandering through aboriginal country. But we come to something much more familiar in the circle within circles, for this is the symbol of the aboriginal tree totem. Yes, but many races and tribes believed that trees were sacred, not only the Stone Age aboriginal. There are Sacred Groves still in isolated portions of Palestine and Syria, and numbers of native races still believe that spirits and life are born in and come from trees. The handsome young god Adonis was believed to have been born from a Sacred Tree. He fell in love with the girl goddess Astarte, who kept evil from the ancient city of Byblos, great trading port of the Phoenicians. You are probably familiar with that tragic love story of the gods. Spirits of fertility were believed to be born in trees by numerous ancient races. It seems strange that our own isolated aborigines firmly held similar beliefs.

But up in the left-hand corner of our drawing surely we have part of a broken link-for this is certainly an uncompleted drawing of a mouthless man. To my idea, this proves that the artist of this particular picture was familiar with the strange drawings of the mouthless men. Perhaps the people represented here drew the mouthless men. Perhaps the mouthlessness was symbolic, or a feature of some priestly or mummy ritual. As to the drawings somewhat reminiscent bf hieroglyphics, on top- well, your guess is as good as mine.

If these people really were they who painted the "halo men", then who were they? Whence did they come, and where did they go? Only the sigh in the farthermost gorges of the Kimberleys gives answer.

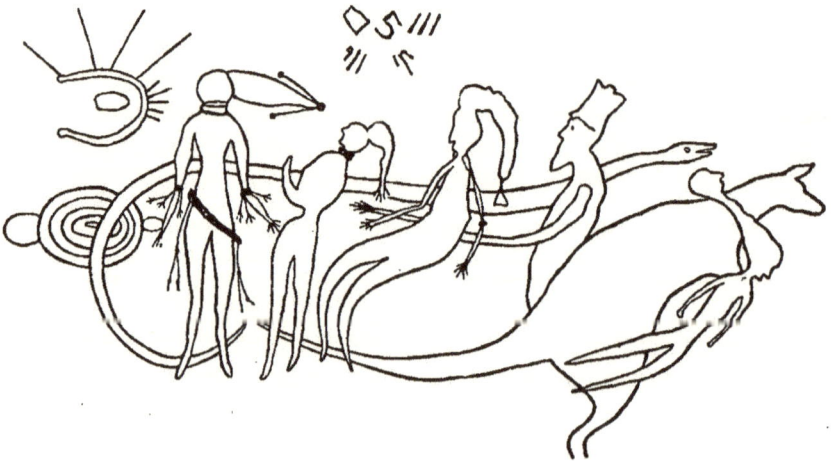

10

AGELESS BELIEFS OF BLACK AND WHITE AND BROWN

WE'LL leave these queer figures and journey on amongst the far better known old aboriginal scrawl drawings, camping awhile along the calm waters (in the dry season) of the Forrest River, East Kimberley. See the photo of a minute portion of a cliff face that is covered in pictures. Can you recognize any of the subjects?

You can see the tiny serpent, and you recognize the emu track, surely; it is like a broad arrow. But what is that queer thing away on the left, shaped somewhat like an anchor? It appears to have an insect's head, or is it a crayfish? A long body and rump, something like an anchor flange, may represent a left leg, while to the right is a definite leg with six or seven toes. What a ridiculous looking thing! A figure farther to the lower right looks almost equally ridiculous. It appears vaguely like a long, thin frog stretched upright. At least one "foot" looks like a frog's foot. But it seems to have some sort of a tail, while the other leg appears quite different, just as the hand on one of the arms seems unrelated to the other. It appears almost as if its left arm is holding out a bow - or is it some musical instrument its weird mouth is blowing? Use your magnifying glass (it is a poor one indeed if not more powerful than mine) and see if you can make any sense of these weird drawings.

Are these the meaningless product of some undeveloped, primitive native mind? By no means. These drawings, and many thousands like them throughout the continent, convey a distinct meaning to those who can read. They represent sacred, spiritistic, totemic, or symbolical subjects. The Australian aboriginal believes that the first beings to come from the sky to earth were half human, half animal or fish or bird. Some eventually changed their form entirely to human; and these stayed on earth and became the ancestors and teachers of the first tribes. These ridiculous looking, human-animistic-fish-reptile-bird drawings portray a tribal belief handed down from the vast antiquity of the Dreamtime.

"Fantastic beliefs!" You smile. 'Weird creations of the primitive mind, but the poor savages knew no better."

But hold a moment! You will see the very same thing in almost all of our own great parks today, statues and fountains that show figures half-man, half-bull-or half-lion, half-bird, half-fish: creatures that never existed in heaven or earth. And these were the products of the great civilizations of the past, believed in as fact, perpetuated in stone and paint. Even today modern civilized people waste money in erecting such phantasies. But half a moment again -

The belief in beings part human, part animal or fish or bird was, and in isolated localities is today, very strong in the aborigines' philosophy of the development of the masterpiece - aboriginal man. Well, doesn't our own science assure us that we've developed from the mud and the sea, from wriggly things and animal forms and monkeys? We can hardly laugh at the aboriginal idea while declaring our own to be "scientific fact". On the other hand, numbers of tribes have an Adam and Eve belief very closely akin to our own. The mind of the aboriginal, although he has never progressed to atomic bombs, has here and there faltered along lines strangely akin to ours.

However, what we are endeavouring to learn is whether there is a meaning in aboriginal drawings - apart from the merely "playabout" drawings, of course. We have already discovered two things that suggest "Yes!" as an answer: (i) The aboriginal artist can draw recognizable humans, animals, birds, reptiles, and fish; and (ii) he can draw symbolical subjects that contain as much meaning to him as our own symbolical subjects do to us.

Examine these photos yet more closely, seek to detect more meanings. And, apart from any Native knowledge you may have acquired, don't forget to bring to your aid any hazy knowledge you may possess of sacred, Lodge, or other ancient symbols and emblematic signs. For instance, St George and the dragon blowing off fire and brimstone would be ridiculous to those who did not know the legend behind it. Think of the numerous old heraldic designs you've seen. Goodness knows what many of them represent, but each had a very vivid meaning to the Family, Tribe, Race, Kingdom, or Nation that Haunted them. During the Middle Ages every robber baron and knight strutted under some such symbol. A weird looking design may be full of meaning to those aborigines concerned.

I'm afraid the very next drawings you see may throw you into confusion, for they consist of lines and circles and curves and meaningless patterns of things. They may contain symbolic, or totemic meaning; on the other hand, they may not. For instance, what does this mean?

And this?

Now, solve this:

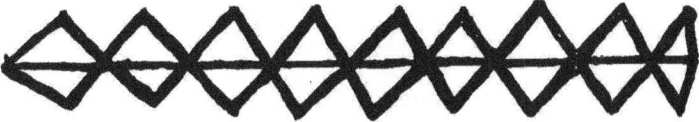

You are getting along well - I hope? Very well, here is the next puzzle:

Yes, that's it. And now you've deciphered the design so far, here it is in full:

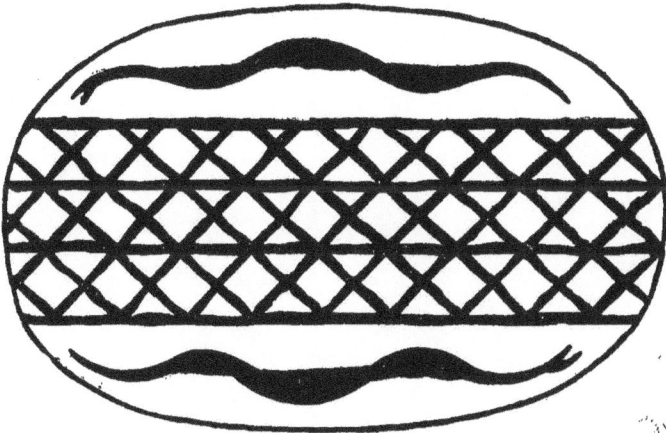

Yes of course, the "alphabet" of the design is simply the spearhead with its barbs.

And this is the pattern the warrior has chosen for his new war shield, a design chosen with as much deep thought as was expended by the chief armourer of old in engraving the sword blade to please the big shot up in the castle. The design shall be the barbs of his favourite war spear! What could be more fitting? The two curly lines burned into each "side" of the design represent snakes, probably signifying that the warrior is a member of the Serpent Totem, and that the Spirit of the Great Serpent will protect him in battle. Many a knight of old thundered yelling into battle with the fervent prayer that the amulet under his tin vest might coax his particular saint to protect him while he slaughtered the other fellow.

Thus we learn that probably every aboriginal drawing, except those scribbled in "playabout", has some meaning.

By the way, here is another exercise to liven up your mind, for there really is great fun (and quite often rich profit) in thinking:

That portion of the cliff face represented in the last photo is now inaccessible except by a very long ladder. Even a lizard would find it difficult to climb to the drawings. How, then, did the Stone Age artists paint such pictures (there must be some thousands of them) away up on a cliff face like that? I have never even heard of wild natives using a ladder.

To make the problem more interesting still, I have seen paintings elsewhere so far up on a cliff face as to be out of reach of any ladder. How did the native artists get there?

If the answer eludes you, then get your schoolboy son to tell you. These modern youngsters can answer most things.

11

THE FINGERPRINT SYSTEM OF STONE AGE MAN

WELL, what have we learnt so far? One thing is that there is a deep mystery in the Kimberley aboriginal cave paintings. Another is that the aboriginal can quite clearly portray the animals, birds, reptiles, fish, that he sees, or that his father's fathers have seen. Another is that he can quite clearly, to those who can read, portray his conception of semi-human ancestral beings who, to his firm belief, came from the skies to populate the earth.

Another is that from a fragment of a weapon he can create a complete design, and embellish it with symbols that lend him added confidence in hunt or battle, and also hope of aid from a power higher than he.

He can create designs, taking his pattern from many subjects, such as the ridgy bark of some particular tree, the markings on the carapace of tortoise, turtle, or crocodile, the tracks of animals. Many such natural things give him the idea for his design, apart from totemic and legend designs.

To proceed in our fireside quest for knowledge in this fairly interesting little subject, let us now learn about "playabout" drawings, thus to be able to eliminate them when we recognize them. Playabout drawings have long encouraged the impression that aboriginal drawings are merely the childish product of undeveloped minds. Many appear absurdly crude, apparently without rhyme or reason, the childish scribblings of an undeveloped race.

Well, the playabout drawings that survive have been done merely on the spur of the moment, or to while away idle hours when a band of huntsmen has been held up by bad weather, or when the whole tribe has been camped near some sheltering cliff face where the game has been plentiful, and the tribe, full bellied, has dallied awhile; or to pass time in a wet season camp. These drawings are just what they are termed, "playabout", at the whim of anyone, or scribbled by all hands in trying to   outdo the sketches   of the artist of the band, in play and joke. So would any dozen of us, if monotonously held up in camp, seek to while away the hours with pencil and paper, making awful drawings to be laughed at and thrown away.

In lots of places in the continent you might ride by a rock face covered with aboriginal scribblings, and pause curiously.

"What name that one?" (What do those drawings mean?) you ask the aboriginal horseboy.

"Huh! him playabout!" answers the abo. and rides unconcernedly on.

Such also the numerous "hand paintings" have generally been believed to be, just playabout, product of an idle hour. From time to time I've seen photos of such "drawings" in the Press, imprints of human hands upon a rock face. This, in "playabout", is very simply done. The artist crunches ochre, pipeclay, or powdered charcoal in his mouth, fills up with water and mixes it; spreads the palm of his hand with fingers outstretched upon the rock face, then blows the contents of his mouth around the hand and between the fingers; holds his hand there awhile until the ochre nearly dries. When he withdraws his hand there is left the clear imprint. More rarely, he squirts the ochre upon the palm of his hand and fingers, then presses the hand upon the rock. For a job made to last, white pipclay is generally used against a black or dark coloured rock, charcoal against whitish rock, coloured ochres against most shades of rock.

These hand impressions are generally considered as "playabout", and very many of them are. But there is far more in it than that. The impression may signify identification or remembrance; it may be a sacred sign, or a sign of guidance, or several of these combined. For instance, such a hand impression, carefully placed, will tell the man's mate, his hunting party, or the whole tribe, that he has been there. This can mean identification, and also news, and can give information in a surprising number of ways to seekers, visitors, or travellers. For a man's handprint identifies him just as surely as our thumb print identifies the civilized man of today.

So the Stone Age Australian aboriginal anticipated the Bertillon system of fingerprints by a thousand years and more. Which is a rather surprising thought. Just as the aboriginal tracker identifies for life, when he has once seen and memorized it, the footprint of a certain man or animal (and even some slight peculiarity in the track of an individual bird), so he identifies a hand print.

I first learnt this as a lad when travelling with aborigines in Cape York Peninsula. We camped one sundown near a mountain summit under shelter of a huge, light-grey granite boulder. While the billy boiled, idly I noticed Big Jacky making his hand impression more carefully than usual on a corner of the rock. He sat back, surveying his masterpiece with satisfaction.

"What name that one?" I asked.

"Me bin tell 'im Chunga which way we bin camp!" he replied. I turned to my half-caste mate.

"Isn't he just playabout?" I asked. "What does he mean?"

"He's dead serious," replied Charlie. "Chunga's crowd will come along here five sunsets from now, and Big Jacky is telling him where we've decided to camp and wait for him four nights from now."

"How does that imprint tell all that?" I asked doubtfully. "Well," explained Charlie patiently, "Chunga is to follow our tracks in five days' time, as we've arranged. That will bring him to this rock. He will recognize Big Jacky's imprint. That imprint is on a corner of the rock that overlooks that particular valley away down there. The direction of the spread of each finger has a meaning in showing where we've decided not to go, while the outstretched middle finger points directly to the big waterhole on the Daintree - where we'll camp and wait for the other parties."

I stared doubtfully at the crude drawing.

"Take a bo-peep along the middle finger," suggested Charlie.

"Hold your cheek to the rock and sight along the finger as you would along a rifle sight."

I did so, and there was a surprising view in mountain-tops and down valleys straight towards where I now saw the big waterhole on the Daintree must lie.

"H'm," I said and straightened up, "but how is Chunga to know we'll be there four sunsets from now?"

"   Because he will know where we will camp as soon as he glances at the direction pointed out by the middle finger. He knows each handy camp where it is usual for a party to camp when making for that waterhole, while loafing along as we are now."

"Well then, supposing something happened so that we could not make the camp."

"Oh, Big Jacky would leave some sign to tell him," replied Charlie patiently, "somewhere handy along the track."

"There's a lot more to be read in it than that," proceeded Charlie. "It tells that all is going well, tells the number of us, and other things."

"The number of us?" I stared doubtfully.

"See if you can read it." Charlie grinned.

I couldn't. Finally I said, "All I see is the palm and outstretched fingers. If each finger represented a man, then one is missing for there are six of us."

"How about the imprint?" grinned Charlie.

"Oh, I see. Of course!" I guessed. "The imprint is Big Jacky, while the five fingers are the other five of us."

"You're learning," nodded Charlie to Jacky's wide grin.

"Well," I said, "supposing we had picked up another party, or even a single stranger."

"Big Jacky would leave a sign to show him too," answered Charlie and spoke in aboriginal to Big Jacky. Jacky picked up a piece of charcoal and made a little scratch below the left-most finger of the imprint.

"There you are," nodded Charlie, "there's the seventh man, the stranger who has joined us."

"That seems simple," I said.

"It is," replied Charlie, "when you know how to read it. Now supposing that Big Jacky had set out alone, with Chunga to follow as arranged. Big Jacky meets six hunters, who join him. Jacky camps here as arranged, and leaves that imprint. Five nights later Chunga camps here and the imprint at a glance tells him that Jacky has picked up six hunters, and that they are making their way to camp at the Big Waterhole on the Daintree."

"That's jolly interesting," I said.

Charlie glanced towards the billy; it was nearly on the boil. "With a few scratches," Charlie nodded at the imprint, "it can be made to mean a lot more than that!" In aboriginal he spoke to Big Jacky who picked up the charcoal again, grinning widely at this flattering interest in his work. With stubby finger he smudged out the charcoal line indicating "the stranger", then rapidly scrawled five upright lines behind the palm of the imprint, and a dot just before the tip of the middle finger.

"Now, read that," invited Charlie.

Falteringly I tried. "The palm imprint means Big Jacky. The five outstretched fingers mean five men. I'm blessed if I know what the dot and the five upright marks mean-unless they mean another five men."

"No," said Charlie, "the five fingers represent men no longer, they go back now more to direction. But those five upright marks *do* mean men. And more-they mean identification! And the dot by the guide finger means something very definite. Now see if you can read them."

After doubtful thought, I ventured a guess. "They mean us. The palm is Big Jacky, the long mark is Big Paddy, one of the shorter marks is Curra, the other the same length is me, the shorter but broad one at the top is you (Charlie had very broad shoulders) and the smallest one is Chulbil."

"You've got it," said Charlie. "So Chunga and the boys with him when they come along will recognize at a glance every man who is with Big Jacky, even if they had not already known. And the dot before the guiding finger means to camp; we definitely will camp at the Big Waterhole. If something had happened by now to disarrange our plans so that we could only camp two nights at the Big Waterhole, then Jacky would have placed two dots before the guiding finger. And Chunga's party then would come travelling swiftly to catch us up, otherwise they'd arrive to find that we'd moved on. And so on. But lessons are finished-billy's boiled."

And Charlie strolled towards the fire as Jacky whipped up the charcoal and made lightning scratches on the rock.

"What's that mean?" I called to Charlie.

"Can't you see?" he replied indifferently. "They're our dogs' tracks."

So again we've learnt something further. That: (i) numerous drawings are "playabout", not to be taken seriously; (ii) occasional drawings, generally believed to be "playabout" are not; (iii) with an imprint and a few scratches an aboriginal can leave a message that conveys not only sentences with distinct meaning, but identification of persons also, and of animals.

Hand imprint identifies Big Jacky. Middle finger points direction. The dot represents "Will camp". The five strokes are broad shouldered Charlie, Big Paddy, Gurra, skinny me, then little Chulbil. The tracks represent our three dogs.

12
THE SIGN OF THE CROSS

SO now we know that an aboriginal imprint and a few charcoal scratches can be read as a message that it has taken me half a chapter to explain. Such was so, anyway, among some of the wild tribes in my day. Unfortunately, I did not follow the matter up. The ideal conditions under which I roamed with that happy go lucky tribe were not to last; for during those glorious years I was ever travelling on. The call of gold and the lure of new country were irresistible to itchy feet; and the reading of a message hidden in a few native scratches was only of passing interest to the scatterbrains of youth.

Thus, the imprint of a native hand often is merely "playabout", but it can represent a vastly different meaning. Here is another fact that I found out only after some years of wandering:

In burial caves there are *no* playabout hand or foot imprints. Such places are as sacred to the aboriginal as our resting-grounds are to us. Hand imprints in a burial cave are for a very definite reason; they are believed to tell the spirit of the deceased that the visitor still remembers him, that he has reverently visited the cave to see that his bones are in order, and to show his respect and love. In a very similar spirit do we tend a loved grave; keep it in order, and lay our remembrance of flowers upon it.

Thus we are increasingly learning that an aboriginal drawing may convey some definite message. We may even think now that we should be able to read a message or two. Ah, it is not so simple as that! So let us go into it a little more deeply first.

Many of the serious signs or messages have, to us, confusing meanings. Fighting and hunting scenes, unless drawn in what we will later term "aboriginal shorthand", are easy for anyone to understand; but other subjects are conveyed in numerous patterns (or symbols), some intricate, of lines and figures, often apparently geometrical. There are circles and curves and dots, squares and oblongs, straight and crisscross lines, wavy and crooked lines, patterns occasionally reminiscent of Egyptian hieroglyphs, their very confusion helping confirm the long-held belief that there is no message in them at all.

Just for the fun of it, as an "appetiser", let us see if we can sort something intelligible out of the following puzzle. Now, what does this mean? It is simple indeed to read:

Simple as ABC. Each sign represents the same. Crossed boomerangs. You've often heard of crossed swords! Well then, the sign of the crossed boomerang means "Fight!"

Now, read these signs:

You have them: I and 2, the new moon; 3, the full moon; and 4 and 5, the sun.

An aboriginal artist of course would represent these simple drawings so clearly that his tribesmen would never confuse a crescent moon with a boomerang, a full moon with a ceremonial, totemic, sacred, or other symbolic circle, or a lizard with a crocodile-as you could easily do from my primitive attempts. However, we are merely attempting to detect different phases of their "art" before rushing in and trying to put meaning into their drawings. If we did that now we should soon give up in confusion, declaring the whole thing just a hotch-potch of nonsense; it would be like asking a man to read Latin when he couldn't even spell his own language.

Now, what do these signs mean?

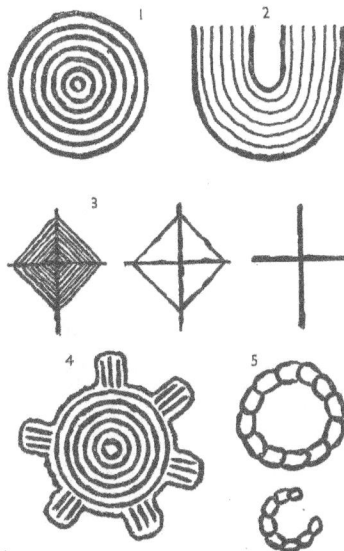

This is much more difficult. You have a partial key to it, though, if you are familiar with the locality, and can learn whether the aborigines attach any special significance to this area. Are the signs on a Sacred or Bora Ground, an Initiation Ground, a Totemic Ground, a Spirit Ground, Burial Ground, some important Corroboree Ground, Youth Initiation Ground, Ground of Earth Fertility: or are the signs well away from such revered or otherwise important localities?

You may get the idea better if I put it this way: Are the signs on a cathedral site, a cemetery, a cenotaph, an arc of triumph, an Anzac parade, an Olympic field, an irrigation works?

For these signs, like many others, carry different meanings according to locality. They may be symbolical, sacred, totemic, or secret. Say the circle within a circle sign is well away from any grounds. Then it is a secret symbol, and your guess is as good as mine. But say it is near a Totemic Ground. Then it is a totemic symbol; it represents a totemic tree; those circles are the tree itself" right to the heart. Imagine you sawed a tree in half: there you would have the design, the markings of the "inner" tree. Within this tree may live, or come to dwell at certain important periods, the Totem Spirit responsible on earth for some great good to Man. For instance, it may be that particular totem super-being that first brought yams to earth, and yearly still influences those good foods to grow in rich crops so that man will not go hungry. (The same would apply to all vegetable foods, to animals and fish, and also to sun and warmth, birth and death, and other things and happenings besides.) Well, the circles in our drawing represent the totem tree, also the people to whom that Totem Spirit is what we should probably call a guardian angel.

An added help to partial understanding is this. Trees in general mean far more to the aboriginal than they do to us, and trees in particular vastly more so. Trees mean "life of the land" to them. Certain sacred trees and groves of trees in particular represent "spirit places", inhabited by the spirit of a certain totem, or by spirit babies awaiting reincarnation into the tribe, or by spirits of ancestors who come from the skies during some very important ceremony to be invisibly present and to visit the tribe's earthly sacred places again. This helps explain one source of the intense bitterness of the aborigines against early settlers who put such sacred trees to the axe and firestick.

A circle within circles, but fewer and much larger circles, may also represent the sun, complete with many rays. Probably you have at times noticed that the sun appears to be a number of large circles, encircled by shadowy rays or a halo. Such is the drawing, a sacred one, that represents a prayer to the Sun Spirit for more warmth, so that the animals and birds will mate and multiply, so that the vegetable bulbs and roots and fruits will swell and grow fat and ripen, so that the poor, hungry Children of the Sun may eat and live. So actually do many aboriginal tribes (or in their wild state they used to) pray to their Deity in the Sun for warmth to ripen the fruits of the earth. If ever you find a drawing such as I have poorly described you will be able to read a wealth of meaning into it.

When I was a lad in Cape York Peninsula, before the first great Spanish influenza epidemic, followed by a second, practically wiped the aborigines out, I saw there another circle within circle drawing, which was greatly revered by a number of tribes. In this, the inner circle, the "heart", was very small, while the surrounding, enclosing circles were much closer together. This one sacred drawing represented the complete tribe, and all their beliefs: one in all, all in one. The tiny inner circle was the tribe itself. Succeeding circles represented their system of life, the degrees of initiation and warriorhood from youth to middle age and beyond that so firmly bound the tribe together. Within was the Circle of Womanhood. Finally, surrounding these tribal circles was the Circle of the Old Men, the tribe's supreme earthly council, representing all the knowledge the tribe had attained.

Then continued other circles. These were of totemic-sacred nature, in order of priority, binding the tribe together (I presume we should call these their "spiritualized" beliefs), sheltering the tribe with their circles of helpfulness. Food and warmth and shelter, continued life and spirit life, and the deepest of their hopes and beliefs all came into this, enclosing' the tribe with continued life on earth, and life to come. I remember, although it is a good many years ago, that the second outer circle was the sun and all that it stands for; while the final circle enclosing all was the sky and heavens and all that outer space stood for to the tribe. Which was a very great deal-far more than I could grasp at the time, even though my half-caste mates fairly often explained it to me. Even now I have only the vaguest notion of their beliefs of the sun, the moon, the stars, and the sky.

In that one simple aboriginal drawing there was rich material for a large book. A crude drawing of a circle within circles may convey a world of meaning to the aboriginal, even so much more than I have been able to convey.

Now, the sign of the U within the U shown in the second figure. This represents the men, and number of leading men, of the particular totem represented: otherwise a tribe, a large hunting party; or a number of animals, or birds. All, when this symbol is used (but remember, only according to my own incomplete knowledge) are represented as resting, or sitting down, or crouching. Men in camp or at a corroboree; kangaroos resting in the shade; plain turkeys at the crouch when flat upon the ground. Such a drawing is almost always, in conjunction with some form of the circle within circle .and other symbols, used on the sacred churinga sticks of particularly the Central Australian aborigines. The markings on such a stick mean ever so much more than a birth certificate does to us; for those few symbols connect the man back to the remote ancestry, totem, and particular spirit beings from which the fathers of the tribe sprang. So again you see there can be far more in a simple abo. drawing than a civilized man would dream of: his hand print and footprint mean far more than our fingerprints, and his churinga stick means infinitely more than our birth certificate.

Now figure no. 3 is three figures, the third being a simple cross.

Each symbol means the same. This is a sacred symbol representing the last of the final initiation degrees. It means death to any unfortunate woman who stumbles upon the Old Men in a sacred place when making this design: not a drawing, but the actual design itself. It is believed to be blessed with a power, for within it is supposed to come and dwell a representative portion of the Great Spirit at the actual moment when the young man steps over the borderline into full warriorhood. The aboriginal's cross means as much to him correspondingly as our cross means to us. There is much more to it than I can explain, for it is rarely indeed that natives will tell anything at all about these especially sacred symbols to a white man, or to any stranger of any colour.

In making this particular emblem, as distinct from its large representation drawn upon the earth, a long human hair string is wound from point to point of the crossed sticks, sometimes completely covering them u.

This same sign seen in a different locality (in portions of North Western Australia, for instance) can, like other symbols, mean something very important, but different. For it is used in a certain corroboree to signify a stage in coming birth. There is some queer correlation in the sign, or signs. The one, in the presence of the Great

Spirit, symbolizes that the lad no longer exists-for he is now a man. The other (referring to birth), in the presence of the Great Spirit, shows that a new life has come.

And now for no. 4. This is another highly sacred symbol, of totemic meaning. If any man or woman not of the totem inadvertently trespasses upon the sacred place when the ceremony is in progress, then the intruder is killed instantly and buried there, and not a word about it is ever mentioned by any present. The air-borne spirit of this totem is supposed to come and dwell in the sign while the ceremony is being performed, and if it is received in all reverence and all goes well, then those of the totem can be assured of plentiful food that season from the hand of the spirit of the totem. That is the story briefly, as near as I could get to it.

In figure no. 5 both the figures have a very similar meaning. This is a totemic emblem, the drawing representing a circle of stones. The actual object is generally a wall of stones, circular shaped, built up two to three feet high, and about four feet in diameter, though sometimes it is considerably larger.

This symbol has to do with the breeding of fish and with the Fish Totem. To ensure a plentiful supply of fish along that river or coast, or at that waterhole, a seasonal ceremony is gravely held each season, and the Spirit of that particular fish, or turtle, eel, or dugong totem is believed to be present. The meaning, in so far as the aborigines would ever explain, strongly reminded me of old-time peoples' beliefs in propitiating the gods. The opening in the second figure faces east, west, north or south, from whichever direction of the heavens the totem spirit is believed to corne to enter the circle. Not all such circles have a similar entrance way.

Once again, what to us would appear meaningless scribbling upon a wall of rock conveys to the wild aboriginal a volume of meaning. It may express an age-old belief; it may convey an urgent message. For instance, a fresh message upon an outstanding rock (a rock belonging to a particular totem) would be visited by nomad wanderers of that totem, who, on hunting trips, would deviate even for miles to glance at that particular rock. If they saw a freshly painted sign upon it like this below, what would it mean?

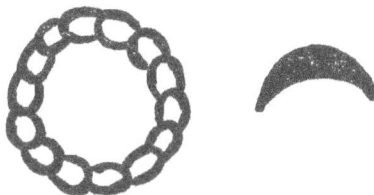

"Gather at the Turtle Totem ground at the time of the new moon." And all of that totem group would make their way there, knowing that some important ceremony in connection with their revered totem was about to take place.

The men concerned read into such symbols far more than I've told you. Their deep inner secret symbols the aborigines simply will not talk about. They may shake their heads and deny all knowledge, they may look puzzled and go dumb, but they won't tell.

Over areas in the Kimberleys, especially in hidden places in that wild bush, are sacred grounds of large area, laid out with stones in sometimes a maze of lanes and passages, circles and squares, numbers of which I've seen represented in cave and cliff paintings. In certain corroborees also I've seen a dance carried out in symbol or symbols that I've seen represented in cliff drawings, and in the patterns of stones on some sacred ground.

Which brings us a step· nearer to the "elucidation of the mysteries". We may as well believe we are trying to solve some deep problem-it's more fun.

What does the simple sign of the Cross read to you? More than you can say: Christ, Christianity, crucifixion, church, priest, parson, wars, conquests, slavery, delivery-and all the innumerable beliefs, stories, hopes, and history of a great civilization.

Remember that for the aborigines a meaning as significant to them is attached to a number of aboriginal symbols, and they recognize those symbols and their meanings at a glance. And, believe me, the aboriginal had invented his crude symbols unknown centuries before Christianity took the sign of the Cross.

13

THE EURO TOTEM

WITHOUT a certain amount of study, of course, we could not hope to "read" the sacred and symbolic drawings of the aboriginal. But merely recognizing that they exist helps us a little farther in seeking a clue to a possible aboriginal alphabet. Now, for something simpler.

What do these three drawings represent?

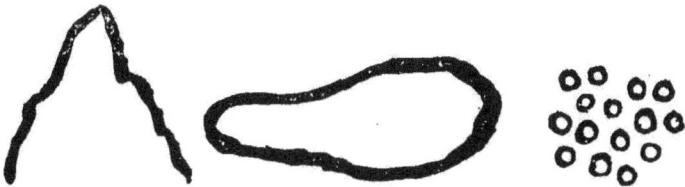

Think a moment. You have seen these three objects many a time, in photo and illustration, anyway.

Here they are:

If you don't recognize my drawings, then they represent a white anthill, a waterhole, and a nest of turtle eggs: which naturally, to the aboriginal, means also that female turtle are laying by night on that particular beach.

However, the aboriginal does not go into detail. The merest scratch, even much less than the first drawing, and his anthill and waterhole are recognized. Furthermore, a scratch beside the drawing with a dot beside it will be read by his friends: "I'm camping at night by the Little Waterhole." Or, with the addition of a couple of crossed scratches which means crossed firesticks (thus a camp-fire), his friends read: "I'm eating at the Big Anthill." If there's a dot beside the crossed firesticks it means he intends to camp there tonight; if two dots, then two nights. A scratch one way or the other would tell his friends he's going to the beach to search for turtle eggs, that he's found turtle eggs, or that he has enjoyed a meal of turtle eggs. I know that the aborigines do "correspond" thus, for. I've seen them pick up a lump of charcoal and scratch that very message.

Despite all the pitfalls, are we game, or foolhardy enough, to believe there may be such a thing as an "aboriginal alphabet" or to try and build one up? Remembering, of course, that the "alphabet" would be in no way like ours, any more than the Chinese is. Older civilizations evolved queer signs, or "picture language", the translations of which defied our scholars for centuries. To the people who evolved them, such signs, expressing their story, are what we may term their "alphabet". However, don't expect an aboriginal Rosetta Stone to be spread out before you.

Now, you can understand these at a glance:

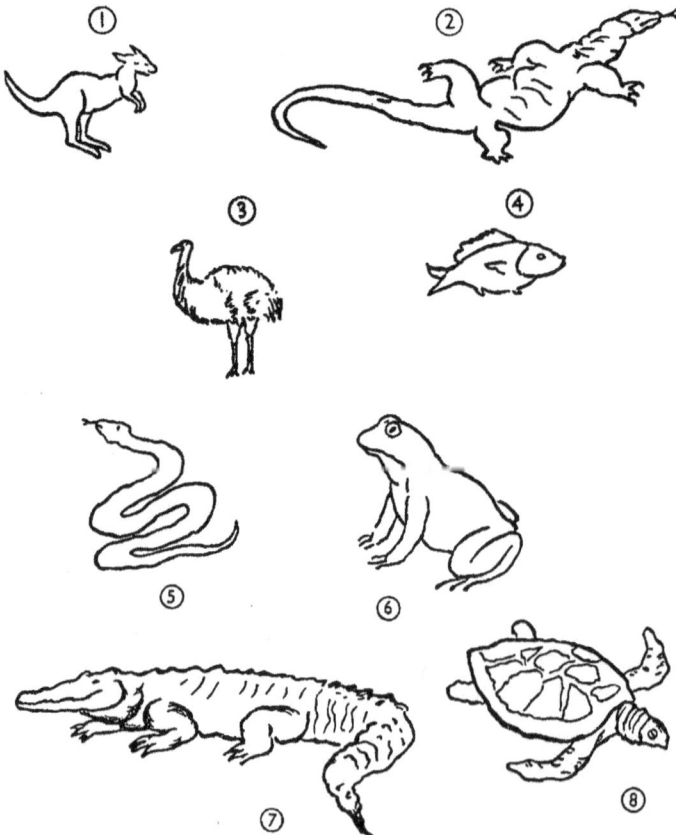

66

Although a capable aboriginal artist could draw all such figures according to nature if he wished, his object is not what we would call a "real" drawing, but more often a mere representation, sometimes a mere scratch or two, which identifies the object to those who see. He can come right down to what, for a lack of a clearer way of expressing it, we may call "aboriginal shorthand", For instance, take no. 2 drawing, which represents a goanna (just as well that cunning, stuck-up creature. cannot see my drawing). For simplicity, we will deal with it as one of the lizard family. Well, apart from a life-like drawing, the aboriginal also represents his lizard thus:

The last drawing represents a lizard's track; so that a line and a few dots not only represent a full-grown lizard but indicate that it has passed that way and was still moving in a certain direction when the huntsman made the drawing.

Take the kangaroo, which comes down to this:

And the emu:

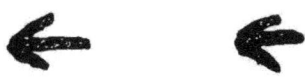

To draw the track of man, woman, child, animal, bird, or reptile is much quicker, and just as satisfactory to the aboriginal as drawing a full man, kangaroo, emu, or dog. And the drawing is instantly intelligible to the aboriginal "reader".

Similarly the track of a crocodile in the mud. What simpler, than with a "paw" as "scoop" to scoop a crocodile track in mud and sand? This can convey where the animal was seen and other facts as well. The track could also be scratched on a cliff face.

Practically any living thing that leaves a track can be so represented. What could be a simpler picture of a dog than this?

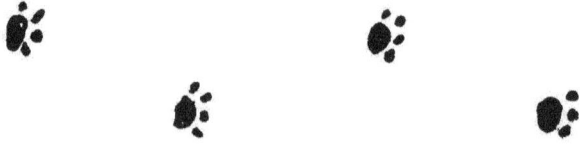

Or a snake:

Or a rabbit:

Could you draw a man more simply than this:

How much drawing would you require to do, to depict a man tracking an emu? And how much skill in drawing would you need to acquire to depict a man with his dog tracking an emu? Here is how the aboriginal artist would depict the story in one:

Thus, you see, the aboriginal goes straight to basic, fundamental facts, with immediate speed and efficiency. The wandering aboriginal boy (no need to develop the skill of a full-grown artist) can leave such a drawing with its instantly recognizable message for his father or tribesmen on a rock or the bark of a tree, for "equipment" merely picking up a piece of charcoal from a burnt-out stump. Or with his finger he can in a moment leave the same message, or a hundred similar messages if· need be, on the sand of waterhole or creek.

Take figure no. 5, the serpent (p. 74). In message drawings the artist would depict it as:
or the track:

In ceremonial drawings it would be like this:
Take figure no. 6, the frog:

The figure on the right you may wonder at, but in aboriginal shorthand it represents a frog. Unfortunately I cannot in those few lines give a true-life representation of a frog as a real abo. artist can.

Take figure no. 7, the crocodile:

The circles in the centre figure tell that the female will soon be laying her eggs. This particular state in the physical condition of the beastie drawn is quite often shown with reptiles, birds, or turtles. Like lizards, crocodiles can be represented by a few lines, or a track, or a few scratches that represent its nest of eggs, etc.

Numerous drawings of a man are made, with or without weapons. From the plainly distinguishable, here are a very few:

Take figure no. 8, the sea turtle:

Again we see, as with the frog, a small figure of a very few lines which perfectly tells the observer all that a large, detailed drawing would. A few charcoal scratches and dots beside it would indicate to those concerned that the party had gone to the coast seeking turtle eggs, also whether such are indicated, and how many night's camp would be made there. And so it goes on.

If you see this scrawl  in a native drawing it means *beche-de-mer*, otherwise trepang, not to be confused with the closely similar drawing of a leech, which has no prickles.

A fish you would always recognize:

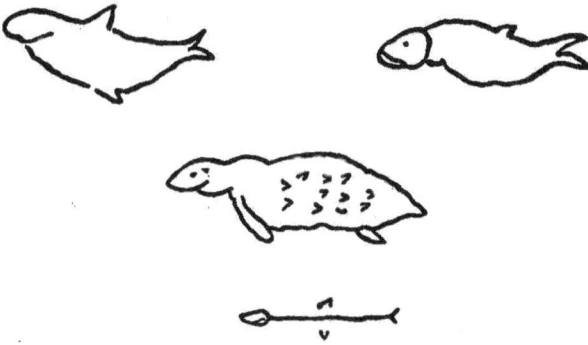

Thus can we claim that the aborigines, or at least some tribes, have or appear to have an identifiable form of picture-alphabet; a picture-shorthand form, perhaps not of writing, but at least of portraying a story to fellow tribesmen.

Four men, five women, four children with their dogs are travelling and have camped four nights. They are seeking fresh-water crocodiles at the Lily Lagoon.

Apart from the very few instances mentioned, with a few lines and a dot or two the aboriginal can portray practically all living things that he sees. He draws the heavens too-not that you and I would recognize these; but his tribesmen do. He can also shorten a shorthand sketch and join it with others similarly shortened so that all together they represent a surprisingly large picture story: the drawing to us being reminiscent of a linoleum pattern of lines, circles and crosses. The aborigines use this shortened shorthand particularly on the limited space of their churinga, and on message sticks, and also on the far larger spaces of their burial posts.

It is generally believed that the markings on a message stick are merely "playabout", meaningless, but this is not so in all cases. I can only say that while I was accompanying a police patrol for twelve hundred miles throughout the wilds north of the King Leopold Ranges, West Kimberley, a number of these message sticks were surreptitiously delivered to both prisoners and witnesses. These were all swiftly translated by members of the patrol, and in each case the message was proved to be fact. Some of the sticks were given us by the prisoners themselves with a broad grin. That these sticks actually gave details of the tribesmen speared, with the names of the killers, seemed to mean very little to the killers who handed us this added information of their "guilt". For to their way of thinking, of course, there was no guilt: these were tribal killings, as carried on by their feud and vendetta laws from time immemorial.

I have mentioned this incident, with photos of some of the message sticks, in Over the Range. So, in message sticks of a serious nature, we have yet another instance of how a few crude lines and dots can mean a long and definite message.

The tribal churinga sticks are revered by any wild, or semi-wild, tribe. Each man has one; it is supposed to be part of him, and it can mean death to him if it is profaned, or stolen from its jealously guarded hiding-place. It is also connected to him by his sacred, secret name, and links him to his ancestral spirit. This deep belief is far too complicated to be further discussed here. Churinga sticks and stones are symbolically carved, with totemic and sacred symbols that mean a very great deal to the initiated. Real churinga sticks are a rarity to the white man, for even detribalized natives greatly fear them and wish to forget them and leave well alone in those most secret hiding-places known to but a few of the Old Men.

I came across a score of such sticks and stones once, by the merest accident, while hunting a wounded euro, away up upon a great rocky tor overlooking a sun-scorched land. Blood spots upon the bare rocks led me up and around to a gloomy fissure going deep into the very crown of the tor. There, on a ledge, while cautiously seeking the euro, I found the sticks. I carried them back to the daylight and was deeply intrigued by their exceptionally elaborate carvings. I should much have liked to have "souvenired" some of those sticks; but by now I knew their priceless value to the owners: to have taken those sticks would have been worse than stealing from a church altar. Maybe it was the totem that finally decided, influenced me. For I recognized in the carvings the totem carving of the euro.

Those sticks connected the humble Stone Age men away in the valley below with the Great Spirit that put life into the first euro far, far away back in the Dreamtime. To this deep, gloomy fissure high up here the Spirit came to brood over his children on those sacred occasions when the Old Men came slowly, reverently climbing up here to croon over their churinga sticks, pleading for rain, and grass, and sun, that the euro might mate and multiply so that others of their tribe might continue to eat and live, praying for the intercession of the Euro Totem that other game might multiply that they themselves might live.

And a euro, of all game, had led me to this sacred place of the Euro Spirit! In that hot, listening silence, there with the musty smell in the mouth of the fissure, it seemed strangely symbolical. The euro lying gasping out its life deep within there had come to its last sanctuary, dying by the bullet of civilization. And away down. below the fruits of civilization was just as surely killing the already fast-dwindling tribe, the Euro Tribe.

I put the churinga sticks back in their hiding-place, and left the euro to die in peace.

14

TOOLS OF TRADE

BEFORE carrying on, here is a little whisper from the past which may interest you. You've learnt that the aboriginal regards his churinga stick as imbued with part of him. It is sacred, closely related to his spirit; it means death to him should it be destroyed.

Well, here is a belief, the *strongest* belief of the ancient Egyptians. They believed that if their mummified body was destroyed by man, or the hand of Time, then their soul would die, cease to live in their spirit world. But - each man, from the Pharaoh down to the humblest, had a *double*. This double was no more nor less than his statue, little matter how crudely carved, but carved in the hardest material he could afford. With the Pharaohs and the well-to-do, of course the statue was carved from the hardest stone it was possible to obtain, and by the best artists. With the poor, it was fashioned from baked clay or the hardest wood obtainable.

Now, so long as this statue lasted, so would last the soul in the spirit land, even though the mummy, the body, at last crumbled away. This statue was part of the man, it held part of his spirit: as the churinga stick is part of the aboriginal, his ancestral spirit reaching him through it. The churinga stick destroyed, and the aboriginal could hold his spirit no more. The Egyptians' statue *double* destroyed and he could hold *his* soul no more.

Now as you can easily understand, the Egyptian paid the greatest attention to detail in preservation of his body, and of his statue double, when he should die. In fact the Egyptian dynasties, for thousands of years, worked almost wholly and solely to this end. If ever a nation lived to die, it was the Egyptians. Most of their work and money were devoted to this end. Which is why the Pharaohs sought to preserve their bodies and their doubles deep down within secret chambers in the heart of those mighty pyramids; why all men who could afford it were buried in tombs hewn deep in solid rock, then solidly filled in. Very strangely, this belief eventually killed the Egyptian civilization, some centuries after the Roman conquest. But enough of that here. It seems queer though, that the belief of the Egyptian in his "double" and the belief of the aboriginal in his churinga should have such strange points in common.

The Stone Age man has lasted longest. The once so mighty Egyptian civilization has gone. Alas, fast going, practically gone, is the day of the churinga.

Well now, back to our aboriginal "artists".

To draw at all, our Stone Age artist had to find materials. He used charcoal, ochres of iron oxides, pipeclays, and kaolins. His colours were black, white, red, yellow. Strangely, he rarely used blue. Yet he could have obtained a blue and a green dye from plants and certain shellfish, and from certain of the copper ores. For brushes he simply cut a length of fibrous vine, chewed the end until it became a brush. For his carvings he used a pointed flake of hard rock, a stone chisel, or a pointed, hardened piece of bone. Yet with these simple materials he has left paintings and rock "scratchings" that have lasted for thousands of years. Time and weathering affect the colouring of the majority of aboriginal paintings that survive. Those that are valued by the tribes are repainted from time to time, and will eventually vanish as the tribes vanish.

There must be a reason for the survival of those paintings that have lasted unknown centuries although never repainted. My own theory, formed because of some slight knowledge of chemistry and minerals, is that the particular ingredients of the paints used in these paintings or drawings were mineralized, or that the paintings were painted on to mineralized rock. The solvent action of water, moisture, aided by temperature would in time spread, by concentration and deposition, a thin film down over the rock face, a mineralized scum as it were, and this would actually "mineralize" the materials of which the paints were made, thus preserving them.

Some proof of this might be sought at Cobar. The local aboriginal name was "Copar", meaning the coloured ochres, richly prized, from which the aboriginal paints were mixed. The aborigines had their own "mine" from which they mined their ochres, which in this case were actually copper pigments. It was through this native "ochre mine", just a brightly coloured hole in the ground, that the very rich Cobar copper mines were found. Several of the northern Queensland copper mines were discovered in the same way.

In such cases, the ochres used by the native artists were really mineralized paints, which would last much longer than ordinary ochres. Then again, if such mineralized pigments were painted upon a mineralized rock face, the paintings would last much longer still.

As to natives obtaining such especially prized ochres when their tribal grounds were hundreds of miles away from such mineralized deposits, they would secure supplies by barter. For it is a fact that the continent was "spider-webbed" by the tracks of barter from tribe to tribe, for pituri and ochres in particular.

Thus the materials and tools. Now the subjects! The earth and all upon it as the aboriginal saw it, the fishes and the stars, his sacred, totemic, and symbolical beliefs. What was his canvas? The cave walls, the cave roof, the open cliff, the overhanging ledge, the bare rock, the tree, the bark, his burial posts, his corroboree grounds (which are like our theatres), his sacred places, the pearl and mussel and other shells, the boabab nut, his churinga and message sticks, his weapons, cooking utensils, his tribesmen and women, and his own skin. He had more of canvas than we have, for he carved in life-lasting symbol and decoration of his own body. He had no actual canvas, though his sheet of treated bark lasted a long time; and his "mineralized" rock carvings and paintings have already far outlasted any of our existing canvases of today."

So the old aboriginal in his crude, primitive way, has been far more of an artist and craftsman than we believe. And he was carving his weapons before and when our ancestors were painting themselves with woad, centuries before our own bold boys carved their battle-axes, shields, and armour. He was carving his rude though efficient utensils, too, as probably all prehistoric men carved theirs. We, of course, have progressed incalculably; the Stone Age men of most other lands have vanished; and our own aboriginal has stood still for thousands of years.

Throughout the continent, the most lasting of native drawings are those in sheltered caves, or upon cliffs where they have been scratched, scraped, or cut into the rock by stone chisels. The numbers and the quality vary in different localities. Some of the most striking are in the rugged areas of the Kimberleys in Western Australia, and in the Flinders Range, that harsh, intriguing range that runs right up through South Australia. These walls of sun-scorched battlements running north and south for three hundred miles are eminently suited for the carving upon and preservation of Stone Age art galleries, not only because of the preservative effect of the grim rock faces, but because of the climate also.

In such places some carvings and drawings must go back for perhaps thousands of years. For here and there not only has the steel-hard ledge upon which the ancients stood to do their carvings frittered away, but portions of the cliffs themselves, the steelhard rock, have cracked and split under untold centuries of heat and cold, contraction and expansion. Here and there, away up on an inaccessible cliff face will be half a drawing, with the remaining fragment fallen far below under some splitting stress of heat and cold and weather and time. Many of the drawings and carvings are so old that the very tribe that once so prized them has long since passed away. Over some of these are carved the symbols of a more recent tribe. The origin of these older drawings is quite unknown to tribesmen living in such localities today, as they were to the remnants of tribes living thirty and forty years ago. At least, to the half-interested inquiries of my younger days the answer was always a blank expression or a shake of the head with a mumble: "Those men lived far away back! Right back in the Dreamtime!"

There must be surprising numbers of such ancient carvings and drawings. The few I have seen I merely glanced at when travelling past that way: useless now to regret that I left unheeded at least one whispering voice from the past. Several bushmen mentioned then that "away out there" upon a sunburned patch of desolation were carved and painted a gigantic kangaroo and emu, and a monstrous thing like a cross between a giant wombat and an elephant. Those drawings may have represented the long-extinct giant kangaroo, the giant emu, and the diprotodon. If so, they would prove that the prehistoric aboriginal lived here in the age of the giant animals. But in those days of the horse and camel, to deviate a hundred miles off the track just to see "a few old nigger drawings" would have appeared plain stupidity.

I've missed plenty of similar opportunities since. Thus we live and learn a little, each concerned in our own affairs as time marches on.

As to the quality of the aboriginal artists, it was much the same as with us. In every tribe there might be two or three real artists - but all hands right down to the piccaninnies had the itch to draw, just as we have.

15
WHERE I AM THE HERO

WE are picking up the tracks a lot more plainly now: in no time we'll be able to read this aboriginal "writing", these picture stories or symbol stories, or whatever they are. But we've been going along too fast: once again we come up against a stone wall. And on this the most ridiculous things are portrayed, things that surely cannot possibly be living, or ever have lived. These are senseless scrawls that could not mean anything even in the mind of the infantile artist. A few of the sketches on this cliff face we recognize straight away, vague animals and birds and tracks. And yes, there are a few of those now recognizable, weird things, half man, animal, serpent or bird, representing the first beings that came to earth. But the rest is all a senseless jumble.

Study closely and patiently. By and by it dawns upon us that, hanging from an appendage from that shapeless thing, is drawn something that resembles a human hand. Correct. The object's identification mark. That thing represents a man. Farther along is another weird scrawl, and dangling from it is what appears to be a tiny foot. You see another very distinguishing mark upon it, and hazard the guess-woman! Correct.

Quite bucked up by this momentous discovery, you try to identify something else. Another shapeless form has a tiny scrawl beside it which vaguely reminds you of the snout of a pig. Correct. That drawing represents a wild pig. Yet another shapeless scrawl has a smaller scrawl unattached to but beside it, which looks as meaningless to. you as the larger one. A bushman interested in such things would declare it the pad, otherwise the track, of a camel. So this drawing therefore represents a camel; and furthermore you have learnt something else - that this drawing, at least, was done since camels were introduced to Australia, just as the drawing of the wild pig tells you it was done sometime after Captain Cook landed on the Endeavour River. Believing you are now learning things, you declare that a drawing farther along the wall represents another wild pig

Wrong. Your bushcraft, or rather observation, is not sufficiently developed. An aboriginal would immediately declare that little scrawl beside the larger as the snout of a dugong. And so on and so on, for this type of drawing. Apparently it does not matter how shapeless the scrawl, for there will be some little identification mark attached to, or beside, or near it. For instance, one small line, straight or crooked or wavy, but below, or above, or beside the drawing, is a small mark that is obviously the head of a serpent.

"A snake!" you declare.

Correctly, so, but only in part. For an aboriginal will know by the shape of that wee little head whether the drawing represents one of the giant serpents of their mythology, or an ordinary carpet, brown, black, diamond, python, tree, or whichever snake it does represent. And possibly, but only if it suits him, he will explain what each drawing represents, and whether a number of them ate connected into a story.

Occasionally also, you will corne across similar unrecognizable scrawls identified by a small track beside them, of human, animal or bird, or of snout, tail, or fin of fish. Thus the main object of such artists is not to draw a life-like picture of the subject, but to identify it. Which seems to me an easy way, and a very quick way, of drawing. The merest scratch will do, so long as that little identification mark is added. Near such drawings at times, small wavy lines, dots, hooked lines, curves, often contain further meaning to explain the larger drawing, or connect it with a "story meaning" to other drawings.

So we learn yet a little more. Shall we number what points we have learnt of the puzzle so far?

1. That there is a mystery in the Kimberley cave paintings.

2. That the aboriginal artist can draw recognizable humans, animals, birds, reptiles, fish, weapons, utensils, and various natural subjects.

3. That he can portray subjects in symbolism.

4.bThat from a fragment of a weapon he can create a complete design, and further embellish it with symbols complete with meaning. (He can do similarly by taking the carapace of a turtle, the ridgy back of a crocodile, the markings of a snake, the track of a bird or animal as design.)

5. That he can portray semi-human ancestral beings.

6. That very many drawings are mere "playabout", the passing away of idle moments.

7. That an apparently meaningless drawing may not only portray a story, an incident, or a message, but may also be an identification of a man or men, animals, birds, serpents or fish.

8. That a hand imprint, apart from "playabout" and identification, can also be a sign of love and remembrance.

9. That aborigines also draw symbolical pictures, any particularly

important one of which may contain chapters of meaning to those concerned.

10. That the aboriginal can make a "picture" message, that is, a rough scrawl representing some local place, scene, or corroboree ground. A few scratches representing humans, animals, birds, reptiles, can convey a long, coherent message to those who can read it.

11. That man, animal, beast, bird, or reptile may be drawn from life size downward, or may equally be represented by a small track mark. For instance, the track of a man or men may represent a man or men, or an individual man or party. As a rule, such an imprint or sketch represents a man or men, travelling.

12. That an aboriginal may draw a "shorthand picture" message. Thus a small, apparently meaningless geometrical figure, or pattern, may represent a man, spirit, tree, or animal. With such figures, he can represent his spiritual beliefs, and probably any living thing he sees upon earth.

13. That a tiny hand, animal track, or snout, or ears, a bird track, a fish tail, a crab claw, a reptile's head, are used in some drawings to identify the shapeless scrawl.

So, to our surprise, we really have learnt quite a lot. And we set out now, warily but with some confidence, to read the next drawing we find farther along the track: only to stare blankly at the cliff face. For we recognize nothing in these particular drawings.

Little wonder. For many of us experience difficulty in recognizing the meanings in possibly "similar" paintings of groups of our own artists today. Knowing nothing about art, I'm afraid I can hardly explain this. I mean those "futuristic" or "abstract" paintings, those queer things of cubes and circles and whirls that are, apparently, complete pictures in the mind of the artist and his friends, but that are a complete mystery to the ordinary looker-on.

Well, here and there among the abo. artists there have been some who have developed this class of drawing. The artist can see, in his mind I presume, the theme which his picture represents. So can a few among his tribesmen when he explains it. But I've got an idea that the majority are just as puzzled by such drawings as we are when trying to unravel a similar painting by one of our own race.

I have told you all I know about aboriginal drawings what I don't know would fill a book. Perhaps you'll become sufficiently interested now though, to gaze with more curiosity upon any aboriginal rock drawings you may chance to see upon your next holiday. Many are to be found near the capital cities; thousands are known around Sydney alone, by the few enthusiasts interested. Unknown thousands have been obliterated or built upon. I know nothing about these very numerous southern drawings and carvings, but it would be a good idea if the most interesting of them could be protected and preserved for the benefit of future generations. No doubt they would take far more interest in these fascinating relics from our voiceless past than I have. For remember, as Times goes gliding on into the centuries, the wonder children of our descendants will be fascinated by any little thing at all that in their own loved country was actually made by the once-living hands of Stone Age Man.

Before going bush to find and "read" native drawings, copy a score of times the few sketches in this book. Thus you will quickly memorize and learn to distinguish them. If you're not sufficiently interested, then set the youngsters at the job. They'll take to it, and it could set them on the way to learning effortlessly quite a lot about nature and the world around them. Having memorized these signs, and added the "civilized" horse, cow, pig, goat and as many others as you can think of to your collection (you and the kids will be surprised at how quickly you will learn to "shorthand" such sketches and pick up many of the tracks) then take the family down to the beach as usual. Or down to the river fishing if you're in the country.

Then try yourself out by telling aboriginal picture stories in the sand. You'll surprise yourself. And Mum, too. For once you'll be useful, taking the kids off Mum's hands and giving her a bit of peace.

The aboriginal, with the greatest of ease, can entertain not only the family but the whole tribe by "telling stories in the sand". Just squatting there, talking steadily, ceaselessly illustrating the story in the sand by lightning movements of fingers and hand. With finger tips, fingers, thumb, ball of thumb, palm of hand, and butt of palm, he can draw any attitude of man, animal, bird, reptile, fish, or tree to perfection. He first smooths the sand beside him, then quietly carries on with the story. With one movement, it seems, a picture is sketched-then Battened clean again with a smack of the hand as he carries on with the story. Many a time I've watched this. Not only does it entertain the kids, but it is yet another aid in teaching them to recognize tracks and natural things, and it encourages them to tell sand stories themselves, to widen their education, and to learn to use their heads.

Perhaps a story from memory will show you how it's done. First the scene: Eventide. The sandy bed of a large creek. Blaze from the camp-fire illuminating the waterhole, shining on the laughing eyes of the piccaninnies crowding round. The camp well sheltered by the steep banks and heavily foliaged trees. Away around us, the black gloom of mountains of the Bloomfield and Daintree. We have rejoined the tribe after a recent wild pig hunt. And now old Dunabril, a twinkle in his eye, squats there telling the picture story of the hunt. With a few lightning flicks of a fingertip upon the sand he has pictured the eager huntsmen gathering round, the tracks of the dogs, Norman and Charlie getting their rifles as we declare that the warriors with all their spears will run for their lives if an old boar charges us. With a little special care he sketches Watchel Jack (me) reaching for my rifle - just a couple of flicks of the finger-tip. But there is something comically life-like in that stupid little mark in the sand and I know full well it is me. I don't need the piccaninnies glistening eyes, their rapidly growing interest, their wide grins all ready to break into shrieks of laughter, to tell me that I am going to be the "star actor" of this story. The goat, in fact.

With a smack of the hand the pictures are wiped out as old Dunabril's soft voice carries on with the story. A rapid "run" of his finger-tips showing the eager dogs' tracks plunging ahead into the jungle, Norman, Charlie, and the huntsmen following, me there, too, stepping out bravely, the rifle prominent, *very* prominent. Tiny marks that represent the wretched leeches, then a ludicrous figure, me, with leg stretched up scraping off the bloodsuckers.

One movement and the pictures are drawn over and Dunabril's fingers are pressing out pig wallows in the sand. He is sniffing fiercely as his fingers make the dog tracks where they are eagerly sniffing the wallows for fresh pig tracks. Ah! and more slowly now he draws, "digs" out a much larger wallow, with a great intake of the breath sighing, "Rungooma!" (Rungooma, a notorious old boar. He had disembowelled one man, crippled several others, besides killing a number of dogs.)

And just didn't old Dunabril hold the attention of his audience now! A rapid run of the finger-tips and the dogs were seeking Rungooma. As he flicked out the drawing Dunabril howled several times and we all heard the dogs baying way down in the jungle where they had the man-killer bailed up. And there he was too! Just a pressure of the palm on the sand, flicks of the finger it seemed, but there was the distinct outline of the flange of a giant fig-tree, deep against the butt of which the boar had backed his rump and, thus protected, faced the dogs. Another Hick gave the impression of a pig's snout, then the two big, curving tusks. I knew that old wretch Dunabril, as all the audience, was concentrating on those tusks. For of those two murderous things, and me, he was making the story.

Thereafter, Rungooma and his action, to the entire recognition of and satisfaction of the audience, was represented by those two monstrous tusks. A rapid semicircle of the baying dogs' tracks facing the tree flange, tiny figures with outstretched legs fitting spears to wommeras, Norman and Charlie and me with rifles to shoulder trying to get a clear shot amongst the vines without hitting the dogs. All was swiftly portrayed as the now excited old voice carried on with the story. The throwing of the spears, the dogs leaping in, the howling, tearing struggle. A vivid picture from that expressive voice, the merest yet uncannily recognizable finger-tip sketches on the sand. A savage wound to Rungooma, his furious disembowelling of a dog then-the charge. Just those two huge tusks at expressive angle. The silly sketch that was me - a lightning dab - expressed me wildly pulling the trigger, then Dunabril's finger with bow-like impression had me ridiculously tumbling over backwards as I ran (and, believe me, I had run) - on this artistic occasion to hilarious shrieks of laughter from not only the piccaninnies but the whole wretched tribe.

On the real occasion I tripped over lawyer-vines and frantically rolled under some heaven-sent leaning log. And there was the log scratched by Dunabril's finger on the sand, with me squeezing ludicrously under it, and just those two big tusks rooting under. But so suggestively drawn were those scratches that I shivered in memory.

Old Dunabril told "The Slaying of Rungooma" many a time, always to eager audiences, in picture story upon the sand. That story was also "played" in ludicrous corroboree many a time, with eager rivalry amongst the "star" actors of the tribe to portray the part of "Jack", which was me, the goat. I wrote of this incident years ago in *Men of the Jungle*, but always wished I could put into the written story what that old aboriginal put into his expressive voice, his rolling, startled, surprised eyes, his apprehensive, relieved, tensed and comic expressions that so vividly coloured his cunning sketches upon the sand.

Many a time I've watched the old storytellers "tell" such incidents upon their "writing paper", their sketch board, the sand. Try it out, see if you can gain and hold a similarly appreciative audience. As I have said, your skill will interest the kids, teach them powers of observation, and also help Mum. With young Tommy for instance - or whichever little wretch is sure to be sneaking out towards dangerous water when The Eye is off him. Draw Tommy with your finger. If he's got an upturned nose, or a pug nose, or a cauliflower ear, then concentrate on that to identify him to the delight of the other kids. Then with "heel" and palm of hand and finger-tips draw his tracks sneaking away towards the forbidden water area. Rub that out, then with the forefinger as pencil, rapidly draw Mum bawling out to the truant to return. An open mouth (a big one) and "hank of hair" will be sufficient identification if you're clever with your finger upon the sand. You won't flatter Mum, of course; but if you're ambitious show her eyes sticking out like pickled onions, or show her with a threatening stick in her hand. You'll delight the kids and they'll follow the story perfectly. When Mum yells, Tommy races for the beach, of course. As you're talking rub the picture out and rapidly with the finger-tips dot Tommy's progress running for the water. He splashes into it. Rub it out, draw curved lines as you explain the dangerous undercurrent coming in towards Tommy, hungry to drag him out and drown him. Tommy goes farther out, the undercurrent grabs him-you draw the rapid line showing him being dragged out to sea-then you can put in Mum running howling to the water's edge if you like, just the nose and open mouth, but above all the egg-sized tear drops. Rub it out before Mum does so. Then - here's your masterpiece! rapidly draw the dorsal fin and tail. Rub it out. Then draw the open mouth and fearsome teeth-scare the daylights out of little Tommy. Then draw the soles of his feet, make a frantic story of the outspread toes disappearing down the shark's mouth. Then with a spank of the hand the picture is stamped out as you groan hollowly, "Finish, poor Tommy!"

In no time the kids and their friends will start their own picture stories. Challenge them to draw the track of a seagull walking along the beach, or of a crane by the river edge. Laugh at the result, but in a matey way. Then advise them to find the bird tracks and study them, to draw the tracks in the sand until they are recognizable.

In no time they'll be "making" the dog's track; the cat's life will be a misery until they get his track. They'll be surprised to learn of the difference in a girl playmate's track to a boy's, the difference between that of a cow and a goat, a pig and a horse. There are innumerable little stories you, and they, could put into such "sand pictures". It's good fun, anyway, and fun in which the youngsters would constantly be learning something (not to mention your high and mighty self). To the more observant and curious ones amongst them it could well mean the start of developing powers of observation and concentration that would stand by them well during later life. Which was exactly the reason why the wild aboriginal friends of my bush days neglected no opportunity of training their youngsters, from the toddlers upward.

Firstly, though, train yourself just a little. For a youngster is more critical and more devilishly cunning than we generally suppose. If you were proudly to draw an emu track that was a poor imitation of the backyard rooster's, a child's light-hearted criticism might cruel your artistic ambitions for all time.

Try a rabbit track for a start, just the tips of two fingers pressed in the sand, followed by two more. Then a dog's track "chasing" the rabbit. Tip of thumb pressed in sand and "screwed around" just a little bit represents the pad. The finger-tips supply the four toes in a semicircle. For reality, put a scratch or two by the toes, to supply claws.

Be cautious though with cars and aeroplanes. These can be similarly "drawn" of course with a flip or two of the finger. But you've got to have "that touch" or some practice to make such contraptions recognizable. The youngsters of today know oceans more about such modern gadgets that I do. I've got a jealous and very suspicious regard for the mechanical knowledge of the modern kid.

Just out of curiosity we started off to try to learn whether there is more in the crude aboriginal drawings than there appears to be. We have learnt that there certainly is a lot more; but it is now up to you to draw your own conclusions as to how much.

16

IN WHICH WE SEEK MYSTERIOUS SECRETS

COME with me upon a grand adventure. Not to unknown lands or forgotten isles, but to explore far greater mysteries - slumbering miracles within the mind. Mightier secrets await us there than have been found by all the explorers of land and sea, than by all the scientists.

You think I am joking. Not so. Come exploring. Not with horse and tent, car and alpine stock, launch and maps and compass, your plane to pierce the sound barrier and venture on to Mars. We may find greater wonders, while all you need bring is your thoughts. Use these, they can carry you over the earth, and under the sea, and away into space, and through time. In your thoughts, distance means right before your eyes and at the same instant ten thousand miles away; speed means the ageless slowness of the weathering away of rock, and the flash to a hundred million miles within a second.

For a start, muse on mental telepathy. Wouldn't it be handy if you could simply flash a thought to your wife that you couldn't be home for dinner because of a pressing business conference! Just like that! Instead of having first cautiously to think out the excuse, get the number, ring up, then hang on while she is gossiping over the next-door fence. It would be so easy. Just concentrate on her a second, then flash the thought, "So sorry, dear! Can't make it tonight for dinner. The wretched Directors have called an emergency conference and I won't be able to get away until all hours!" Then immediately "tune off" from home and attend to the business on hand.

So simple. You'd "catch on" to your wife no matter where she was, nor what she was doing. No need to fumble with a clumsy, time wasting, out-of-date telephone; no need to hang on and convince her that her suspicions that your "conference" really means. a night at the club with the boys is base and groundless. The matter is finalized in a second: no halting explanations, no wrong numbers, no repairs and telephone bills to pay either. And no back-chat. For you immediately switch off your mind from home and your wife cannot "break through" until you oblige with a receptive mood. A blessing for her also. For when she gets rid of you after breakfast she can relax and gossip to her heart's content with the daughter or friend, even if she is thousands of miles away overseas.

A few moments' thought will convince you that you would thus do away with all our expensive, clumsy methods of communication. Do away with the post, and telegraph, the cables and letter-writing and wireless. What vast expense, time, and labour the world would save, or put to better use!

You could merely sit in your office, at home, anywhere, and tune in with business heads here or abroad, and thus transact business immeasurably more easily, quickly, and satisfactorily. Or personal affairs. When walking along the street, you could get in touch with Bill, Tom, and Harry no matter whether they were here or in Timbuctoo; no need for them to be wasting time at the end of a telegraph wire or phone or mail box. Just tune into Bill's mind, enjoy a chit-chat, and learn all that's doing, merely while rolling a cigarette, or waiting for the tram.

How easy for the engineer of a big construction work to keep in touch with his men; or for the station man to question his travelling drover! The man lost in the bush would merely "telephize" the nearest police station-as you would do if your car tumbled down a gorge. So long as your mind was not "killed" you'd get immediate speedy help. You could think out countless ways in which mental telepathy could be of incalculable benefit to you and the human race.

Right then. Now we start our exploring, to find out if mental telepathy is possible. We'll have little help from science, which is too busy with the high explosive or poison gas or atom bomb of the day. A very few investigators have given a very small amount of attention to the question, with encouraging results. Long ago I became curious, then convinced, about mental telepathy, when I was cruising as a lad among the Torres Strait Islands. We were ashore at Eroob (Darnley Island). We had taken aboard old Maino, Mamoose of Warrior Island, and his quiet, gnarled old henchman Dabor, who seized the opportunity of a courtesy visit to Eroob. We had barely landed at Eroob when I became aware that something of grave import was brewing. Several old greybeards of Medigee village were in earnest conclave with Maino and Dabor. Presently Dabor stood up and, walking slowly to pretty Medigee beach, squatted down with his back to a palmtree, stared out over the quiet waters for a while, then drew up his knees, laid his hands with locked fingers across them, bowed his forehead upon his hands, and was motionless for some twenty minutes. Slowly then he stood up, seemed to gently shake himself awake, walked back to us. He nodded to Maino, then said in the soft island language, "They sail with the midnight tide." The facts were these:

Old Kebar was dying, sinking fast. He felt a great longing to see his only son. He was sure he could hold out if only the boy could be contacted, and asked to come to him. Young Sarkep, his son, was a crew boy aboard one of the Thursday Island pearl-shelling luggers. It was just possible the lugger, with others, might be in Thursday Island to unload shell and take on stores, for she had been at sea on drift three months. But-there was no one aboard that lugger with whom any man of Eroob could make contact. Was it just possible that Maino might be able to do something?

Yes, Maino could. Through Dabor, who could make contact through Pasi.

Now understand the position. Eroob Island lies, as the crow would fly, some one hundred and thirty miles just north of east of Thursday Island, which is the tiny centre of white civilization. The only means of communication was by sailing vessel, no such thing as wireless then, of course. Some forty miles north of Thursday Island is Badu Island, and from here, yesterday, Maino knew the Badu Island lugger was due to sail to Thursday Island for stores; it should be there now. Pasi had promised himself a trip aboard the lugger on holiday bent; and he was the key to the situation, for Dabor could "contact" him. If only Sarkep's lugger happened to be in port, or due, then Pasi would meet the lugger and tell the boy. Whether or no, he would then make contact with Dabor.

Which is precisely what happened. Dabor sent a telepathic message to Pasi aboard the Badu lugger which was then anchored at Thursday Island. The boy's lugger, with part of the pearling fleet, had sailed into port to unload shell and take on stores only two hours before. Pasi rowed across to the lugger, and transhipped the boy to the Badu lugger, which then sailed, while Pasi sent his message back to Dabor. Wind and tide being favourable, the lugger hove in sight off Eroob shortly after midday next day. The boy was in time to farewell his father, while I was very puzzled and surprised.

In subsequent trips among those isolated isles I had occasionally a similar experience. And eventually I learnt that, though a few among the Islanders possessed the power in varying degree, it survived only among the last living members of the old Zogo-le, the priesthood who possessed the developed power of sending and receiving. They had been trained thus from boyhood, through some queer, well-defined culture from a long dead past. (Is the past ever dead?)

The past has left its imprint upon those jewelled isles in Australian waters, apart from the fast-vanishing culture of the dying Zogo-le. For three parts surrounding Eroob there still stands firm the Great Sai. Almost fencing the island in, this stonewalled fish-trap surely must be the greatest in the world, built of coral blocks that must surely have been cemented. But how? The big wall has openings, well placed in relation to tides, which invite fish to numerous further openings in smaller walls, which lead into a carefully thought out maze of pits. The fish come in with the tide as it rolls over the gigantic Sai. As the tide recedes, the fish are left scattered all over the maze of the walled pits that still have water in them. Some pits even trap turtle, and an occasional dugong. When the Islander desires fish for breakfast, he merely strolls down to these pits that have belonged to his family for centuries, and leisurely spears what fish he fancies. Those great walled traps, built out in the open sea, have defied the storms and cyclones of centuries. What vanished people built them? With all our knowledge and modern engineering we have difficulty in erecting an ordinary breakwater capable of withstanding the ravages of the sea.

From the long past, people of every nation have reported instances of mental telepathy. Apart from a distinct word message being received, some folk suddenly become aware of a "thought form", that is, a thought picture of another person or another scene Bashing across the mind. The "vision" may hardly register before it is gone, leaving the receiver puzzled, wondering perhaps whether it was imagination.

On the other hand, a perfectly definite picture message may be received, and the "thought form" person or scene or happening instantly recognized by the receiver. At that precise time that person's mind must have been attuned to receive that message; and it must have been sent purposely, and probably urgently, by some other mind.

Perhaps the receiver completely disbelieved in, or was unaware of, the possibility of mental telepathy, yet saw that picture message because his mind was attuned at that moment to receive such a message. Even if the "picture person", the scene, or the event was unrecognized, it still must have existed somewhere, and been sent and received through the unknown laws of the mind.

So we've learned one little thing here: that it is possible to receive mental messages not by words only, but by "pictures" in the shape of thought forms. In fact, the mind carries not only its own radio, but its own television set. And perhaps it has radar equipment as well!

Puzzled folk have received "impressions" that have later been proved to have happened. They feel "impressed" by a distant person's dim presence, or are conscious of some shadowy happening, or feel urged to take a certain form of action. You have surely heard of a person receiving a warning in this manner? Numerous such instances have been recorded. Other people have been strongly "influenced" about some happening, or event to come, without absorbing a picture, or receiving a definite message. In the course of a wandering life I have met people who tell me they have received messages in which the sense of smell has been the determining factor: a confused picture message in which a tang of the sea has brought realization; or the scent of a rose. In one case it was wattle trees flourishing along a hillside. In another case of a jumbled picture message a faint but definite smell of drying tar brought sudden identification.

Within this workaday mind of ours there lie mysterious, undreamt of powers. If only we could bring them to the light of day, then learn the laws that govern them, surely then we could make them work for our good. We must try to solve the mystery of these powerful, secret things; we must discover what they are and how they work so that we can use them for our own good.

Happy years ago, away in wild bush between Ebagoolah and the Coen in Cape York peninsula, my mate Dick and I were prospecting for gold. In this mild midday, hungrily we had eaten of damper and salt beef washed down by strong, milkless tea, then luxuriously stretched out on our corn-sack bunks for a pipe before returning to the work we loved so well. It was warm in the tent, the midday drowsiness spreading all over the wide, clean bush. Tommy, our horseboy, was away down the creek supposedly looking after the horses. Tommy was a bright, mischievous little aboriginal boy of whom Dick was very fond. As a child, the boy had "adopted" us, rejoining us whenever we travelled through his tribal country. He thought our great dog, Bully, and Dick were the most wonderful things in his world.

I was hovering on sleep when Dick jumped up shouting, "Tommy's broken his leg!" and rushed out of the tent.

We found little Tommy lying all twisted down on the bottom of our prospecting shaft. He had broken his leg all right; he had slipped and fallen. He'd had a boyish idea of playing a joke on his hero, Dick, by tying the windlass rope to the timbering in the shaft so that when Dick went to haul up the bucket he would feel it immovable.

When we'd fixed up Tommy to the best of our rough ability, I asked Dick:

"How on earth did you know he'd broken his leg?"

"How did I know?" replied Dick sheepishly. "All I know is I was half asleep and I felt an awful crash and knew I'd broken my leg-then I knew it was Tommy's leg broken, not mine!"

And Dick could never explain any more.

The way I saw it, even at the time, was that when leaning over the shaft the little aboriginal's mind must have been full of Dick and the great joke he was going to play on him. As he slipped and fell, his mind must have "frozen" on Dick, and Dick, his conscious mind quiet in near sleep, must somehow mentally have felt the crash and the stunned feelings of his mischievous little friend.

Possibly you have heard of other similar instances. Certainly many others have been recorded. Distance does not appear to count in the matter. In fact, both time and distance seem to mean nothing to the mind. After all, it is only man, because of the limitations and clumsiness of his labouring physical body, who has invented time and distance. What he means by these words certainly affects his cumbrous physical body, but is meaningless to that other tremendously important part of him, the mind.

I believe that the reason why my mate Dick so definitely received the message and feeling of Tommy's plight was that at that precise moment his mind, or sub-conscious, or whatever particular comer of the brain it is that is adapted to receive such messages, was in a state of receptivity. And this rule seems to apply to ninety per cent of such cases. Probably to all. After a long and hard morning's labour, we had eaten hungrily, then sprawled out to smoke a pipe of rest and quietness, Presently the peace of the bush, the warm drowsiness, began to lull Dick off to sleep. Gradually his conscious mind lifted away from its load of feverish thoughts of gold and solid work, of the necessity of winning gold to pay the storekeeper's bill and to buy us two more urgently needed packhorses: his mind was slowly beginning to "cool down" and rest, as the muscles and sinews and back and lungs of his strenuously worked body were resting. The subconscious mind, or whatever it is, became unburdened and free to receive the shocked and tensely emotional and concentrated thought of Tommy as he slipped, fell, crashed, tuned in to his beloved Dick and transmitted the overpowering feeling of his twisted leg. For physically his mind of course would have felt it all, and that mind was concentrated on Dick - whose subconscious instantly translated the feeling to his conscious mind, drastically awakening it. And, as the mind acts on the body, Dick felt the fall down the shaft and the crash and the numbing twist of the leg. I'll swear he was quite unconscious of what he was doing as he leapt up shouting and rushed out the tent door to run straight down the creek to the shaft.

Afterwards, Dick of course could no more consciously "fix" his mind to receive a telepathic message from anyone than he could fly. But the fact that nature had done so on this occasion goes to prove that the power is there.

17
THE SLEEPING POWER

Now, are *you* doing your job, thinking with me? If so, you realize that there is actual *power* in human thought. The little blackboy's agonized thought caused Dick's *physical* body to leap into action and continue running through the bush right down to the shaft, straight to the right place. Give that seemingly miraculous action some consideration: there is some form of thought that can urge into action not only your own but *another* body; that can make it do the *right* thing, even when the brain of that physical body is not conscious of what it is doing.

Think about the implications of this, and presently you will realize that this same power must "automatically" move vast tonnages of bodies of flesh and bone every year, making these bodies do the *right* thing for their own good. If only each and everyone of us could use this power within us to our own good! Not only our mental, but our physical good!

Medical science has made many vital discoveries since those happy Cape York Peninsula years. To aid us in our quest, that we may understand what we are looking for a little better, let us take note of a very few interesting things they have found out about the brain. For somewhere within that brain reposes the mind, which is practically the You in you, and the Me in me. Without what we call, and feel to be our minds we'd be useless anyway; we'd only be lumps of meat on legs. Somewhere within this mind of ours hides the comer wherein lurks these vague telepathic powers, and it may help our exploration of that hidden comer a little if we get even a glimpse of brain, consciousness, and mind.

Our brain, the "meaty" part of it, is composed of some thousands of millions of nerve-cells {you did not think of such numbers within your grey matter did you?), and the magic and mysteries of those cells we have not been able to probe in thousands of years. Each cell has grown a long, minute fibre: liken it to a telegraph wire, if you like, for it is along this that nerve-impulses fly to the cell, hence the brain, the mind, creating your feelings and knowledge. Each cell is connected, one with the other. Try to imagine such a vast, complicated, interlocking, extremely efficient, physical-mental-psychic controlling machine, ceaselessly working within the skull of your much larger body. These sensitized impulses work on the brain through the senses so that the mind sees, realizes, hears, reasons, feels, tastes, giving us consciousness, thought, awareness and all that Man is: Enabling the You in you to do things, to realize and appreciate what to us is life.

Have you ever thought about it? If it was not for the fascinatingly intricate and miraculous mechanism that "works" these five things we call senses, we should not know or be aware of anything. We could touch things, but would not feel them. We should not know whether it was daylight or night, for we should see neither sunlight or dark; not know, either, by the warmth of day or cold of night, because we would not be able to feel. A cannon could explode beside us, but we'd not hear it, nor feel the vibration of explosion, nor smell the acrid odour of the explosive-we simply would not know. You could taste neither food nor beer, so would need neither, which would make living very inexpensive. Silly isn't it? But then you would feel very silly without those five senses - only you would not be able to feel.

We do not, in fact, possess the knowledge to realize how fantastically wonderful man is. And we rightly feel humble at thought of the Unknowable, the Mighty Engineer who created us strange beings.

It is through nerves from all over the body, Bashing their magnetic-electric-chemical messages to the deciphering brain, that our five senses operate: The sense of sight by which we see, the sense of touch, of "smell, of hearing, of taste-and the "knowledgeable" portion of the brain that "realizes" what our senses record. The realization of these five senses and their combinations are practically us: we shouldn't be much use without them, for we should comprehend nothing. Think what a terrible handicap it is when a poor unfortunate loses one sense-the sense of sight; then think of the plight of a human who lost the sense of sight, hearing, touch, smell and taste. The human race would not have existed, of course, had it not been for the development of these five senses and the marvellous brain which in a Hash makes us aware of them as they act in their inextricably different ways upon what we call *life*. So the Creator of the Universe, the Mighty Engineer who made all things, must be an inconceivable miracle beyond our comprehension to grasp.

Well, we possess, and operate by, and are operated upon by, these five senses. But you and I suspect that we have another or a "by-product" of all five dimly hidden away somewhere deep within the complicated recesses of that so very small, titanic brain. A telepathic sense controlling but dimly realized powers of mental telepathy, hypnotism, psychometry, second sight; almost certainly other unknown, undeveloped senses waiting only to be explored, understood, developed, trained, then used. Don't you feel that way about it? That is what we are exploring for. To try to find out whether unknown powers do really exist within us. And, if so, whether it is possible to develop and use them.

Experts tell us that the nerve impulses Hooding to the brain for analysis (that is, to be made known to consciousness), are chemical-magnetic-electrical; that if we could see into the brain while we are working and thinking we should see it lit by countless rippling pin-points of light; that the electricity used in the brain is infinitesimal. You and I cannot help thinking that "our" electricity must be extraordinarily powerful, for all that-for with it in a second we can throw our thoughts far out into space, away out for hundreds of millions of miles. By comparison, the most enormously bulky electric power-houses built by man can only throw *their* electricity a few miles. So the tiny electricity you and I use in *our* power box must have something. One thing we believe it has is some strange telepathic power, also capable of operating upon the weighty physical body. If so, then we possess another sense.

You know, or would if you thought about it, what marvellous use, generally unconsciously or automatically, you make of each one of your known senses every day. Just think a moment how constantly you are using but one sense that you barely realize you are using-the sense of touch. Hardly a moment goes by but you use it. Think a moment of how you would do your work without it. Then realize that you could hardly live without it. Very well then, these five senses are the most unobtrusive, silent, ever-willing, tireless, most powerful friends we have. In fact, they are Us. If we could prove we possess yet another sense, what a great deal more of our world around us we could comprehend, what added wonders we might be able to accomplish with it! We have already considered what we could do in the way of communication if we could each individually develop the sense of mental telepathy. But that is only one use we could put this telepathic power to; probably we could direct it to help us in ways far more important. Think of the numerous ways you use the power of sight, for instance. Not only for sight alone. You gauge dangers, nearness, distances, emptiness, fullness, denseness, transparency - a million things you use sight for apart from sight itself. Sight actually makes you think. Think about this for a moment, and you'll "see". Yes, we'd probably be able to make far more use of this telepathic sense than merely to wish the brother in New York "Bon Voyage".

But first, we have to prove, if we can, whether we really do possess this unrealized sense. Experts tell us that when we sleep the myriads of twinkling magnetic-electric lights within our brain quieten, die down. Like the city lights, when the city sleeps, though far more so. As the lights go out and the conscious mind sleeps, the subconscious takes over a full-time job, for it must attend and guard the body while it rests. The experts assure us that the subconscious never rests.

On awakening, the conscious mind takes over. This is what we do things with, think and work and plan and live with. And, so far as I can see, deep again within this conscious mind is the mind proper, which seems to me to be the You in you and the Me in me. Try think it out for yourself. Quietly ask yourself, "Who am I?", "What am I?" Try to grasp it - try to grasp Yourself! You'll gradually become aware how elusive you are. The deeper you think the more you'll find yourself slipping away from Yourself, until in chagrin you realize you don't know who or what you are! Neither you do. But neither does anyone else which is some consolation, anyway.

Now, keep this in mind. For it is a sign-post along the track.

This subconscious mind never sleeps. Not only does it look after the body when the You in you and the Me in me are asleep, but it orders the body to do the million things it must do during the day. It is the power behind the throne when muscles lift up your arm and brush a fly from your face, when you stretch your leg so that it feels more comfortable, and do a million other necessary things. It is the power that by a hairs-breadth startles you into a flying leap a second before the car hits you when you are daydreaming across the street.

A little thought will convince you that you are by no means conscious when you fully believe you are. It is a fact that, often in broad daylight, hundreds of people per year of our small population are killed when crossing road or street. In numbers of such cases they simply walk as if deaf and blind-folded straight in front of a car. Others look neither to right nor left. This is because the conscious mind, right at that moment, is not on the job. It is far away, busily thinking of something else, of anything but the imperative need of safely crossing those few yards of street. Those people, though believing themselves wide awake, and in daylight walking across the street, were actually not conscious. Goodness knows how many times the subconscious mind that can halt or move our bodies in a flash has saved both you and me.

What if we possess some unknown power which we could train to help us, or which could urge the subconscious to help us even more than it so miraculously does! This conscious mind and subconscious mind have incomparably more to do with the You in you and the Me in me than we ever imagined.

Here is another sign-post to keep in mind along our track:

Apart from looking after the body in rest and work, it is the subconscious mind that drives the body to resist disease. Do you begin to realize now how valuable this sub-conscious mind is to us, a mind we hardly realize we possess?

Now, could the You in you, the Me in me, encourage, nay help and direct it, to do vital "body work" for us? Perhaps through this strange telepathic power, which we have already proved can act upon the mind (the old Torres Strait Islander and his urgent telepathic message) and also upon the physical body (Dick and the little blackboy). Apparently the secret of this telepathic power is seated somewhere within the subconscious. Hence, if you and I could "call up" and control our individual telepathy, then, through the conscious mind, we could direct it to help the subconscious mend the body when it was ill or hurt. What a truly great blessing this would be! For the subconscious, battling in its own way to cure our ill, would be greatly reinforced by our own conscious mind through this telepathic power driven by our fervent wish.

You've read how the little blackboy's mental telepathy acted on Dick's subconscious mind when his conscious was almost asleep, and forced his physical body to spring into action - the right action, directing that body even to the exact locality. Well, there is a mental power for you, forcing the physical body to definite action, and giving a magical correctness of location. And at that, while the conscious mind was unconscious.

J   ust think it out quietly, deep within, and you'll begin to grasp what we are trying to get at, and become faintly aware of the wealth of possibilities. Then you will realize that the oft-heard saying, "mind over matter", could contain a much deeper truth than we imagined. It is a well-known medical fact that what we call the subconscious very largely controls the body, and helps it, or perhaps constantly urges and "bullies" it, to resist disease.

It is a medical fact also that "nature" is the greatest doctor. The medical man does all he can, then lets "nature do the rest". And this nature is the subconscious bullying the body to get well.

If this theory you and I are "exploring" is correct, then by the power of our own telepathy to our own subconscious through our consciousness, by helping and directing the subconscious in its curative work, the time could come when the human race could defy disease. There may be far, far more in this mysterious telepathic power than we ever imagined. Do you not believe, with me, that if only we could discover the secret of this power that hides somewhere within our minds, then develop and train it and use it, the benefits gained could change the destiny of the human race?

18
FACETS OF THE MIND

SINCE we cannot unearth this mental telepathic power and study and anaylse it to find out just what it is, and how it works, can we prove its existence in any other way, get a line on it in any way at all? Is there any other power in the human mind that even faintly resembles it? Or any natural power of animal, bird, or even fish? For after all flesh is flesh, and what works through the body of animal or fish very probably also works through the body of man.

Put it this way: A diamond is an ugly stone formed of carbon under stress of great heat and pressure. You would not give a brass farthing for a rough diamond if you did not know what it was; you would tread over it and walk by without the least thought. But the trained mind of the trained man picks it up, gloats over it, cuts and polishes it; and then you call the brilliant thing a "fortune". lt needs trained minds to seek within the meaty brain the polished actuality of telepathic power.

Now, a cut diamond has numerous facets, some have sixty and more. Turn it any way you like, there is always a facet, or a number of facets, glistening at you. But each facet is but part of that one diamond. Could we possibly get a line on this telepathic power through some other facet of the mind!

How about hypnotism? Hypnotism is being increasingly used by medical science in the alleviation of pain, and the curing of disease. The procedure to induce hypnotism seems closely allied to mental telepathy. The patient's mind must be "tuned in" as a "receiver", so that his subconscious will be free to receive the suggestive messages from the concentrated mind of the sender. Mental telepathy, hypnotism, psychometry, may be different forms of this same elusive power. Almost certainly they are facets of the one diamond, the diamond of the mind.

What are dreams? We do not know, but we certainly are aware of them. Could dreams be another facet?

Let us seek for other elusive facets, for some other form of this elusive something, even though in other things than ourselves. For life is a wondrous power, and we' are not the only beings that possess it and the wonders that make up what we call Life.

Search carefully and we may uncover another facet. What, for instance, is the apparently miraculous power that guides the homing pigeon on its flight? Nobody knows. And yet the pigeon, like everything else, must obey natural law. At present, to us, it is a marvellous secret, this uneering power that guides a pigeon home even over *thousands* of miles of unknown lands and seas.

If you were thrown into a chaff-bag and dumped out in the bush even fifty miles away from your home, would you be able to walk straight back? Many people would become lost if they strayed only one mile from camp. But a pigeon, caged in darkness deep within a ship, a pigeon that had never been to sea, was taken on a long voyage, then into strange country, utterly different to its homeland. Finally it was released when over seven thousand miles from its home loft: And it found its way back to the little door of its little home in that pigeon loft seven thousand miles away.

Now, how *did* that pigeon do it? What marvellous power does it possess within that tiny head? A pigeon's brain is small indeed, as you know, and almost all its grey matter is busy keeping its body and feathers in order and regulating its workaday life: obtaining food, fighting, love-making, nest building, keeping on the warm side of its scolding wife, near busting in admiration of that wife's eggs, slaving for its young, guarding against cats and hawks and snakes and other enemies. Surely that "compass" department within its little brain must be very, very small indeed - yet again proving the importance, and often the fantastic power, of minute things.

What is this marvellous power? Could it be some bird form of the telepathic power? A facet of the diamond? Nonsensical thought. But we're merely exploring.

We know no more of the secret of the pigeon's Hight than did the Greeks who used them as messengers in the Olympic Games, and the Turks and Egyptians who used them to carry war news when the Crusaders were playing merry hell in the Holy Land. But we *have* learnt this - that by consistent and careful training the pigeon's power can be developed a very great deal. To develop mental powers requires knowledge, concentration and training.

Now, we possess five *known* senses: Sight, hearing, touch, smell, taste. Could the pigeon find its way home by sight? Naturalists assure us that pigeons possess remarkable sight, probably can see ten times as far as humans; so by sight alone, from flying height and by landmarks a pigeon could easily see his way home over a few hundred miles. But he could not possibly see his way home over *thousands* of miles. It cannot be eyesight that "sees" a pigeon home.

Could the secret then lie in its hearing? I know nothing about a pigeon's ears, but it is impossible to believe that it can hear the familiar billings and cooings in its home loft a few hundred miles away, let alone thousands. Still, we must be cautious here, when we remember sound waves and radio. Could it be possible that in the pigeon's head is some tiny "receiver", that when the pigeon is tossed up and released and circles a time or two he "tunes in" to the sounds in his home loft, and is thus guided home?

It does not seem feasible. But then, the sending of a telepathic message over *any* distance to a receiver who has *tuned* in is quite feasible. Not so many years ago and we would have laughed at wireless, at the idea that it might be possible to send messages and sound and music instantaneously over thousands of miles. A dreamer who suggested it would have been called mad by ninety nine out of a hundred people. Yet not only the possibility, but this *fact* has been in the world ever since it became a world.

We must remember, too, that science has now proved that some animals at least can hear sounds that the human ear cannot hear, sounds both in lower and in higher keys. We do not know how many unknown sounds are floating around this world and universe, passing by our "deaf" ears. Is it possible that the pigeon's ear is "tuned in" to catch sounds through wave lengths from its home loft, even over great distances?

When released, there is nothing so much that a pigeon wants as to get home. His wife and family, his friends, his shelter and warmth and good food, all his interests are awaiting him somewhere far, far away. Easy then to imagine him concentrating on "home" when released; as he climbs higher and higher up into the "sound waves", you can almost hear his "mind" calling "show me the way to go home". And this strange, so handy power or sense within his little head always shows him the way, draws him back home as the magnetic north draws the compass needle.

When aloft, when once he has tuned in to his home sense, he does not always fly straight as the crow flies if he is travelling a great distance. It may be that instinct or common sense urges him to conserve his strength. If a storm or bad weather blows across his path, he detours around it, does not fly blindly into it; then he veers back to his home course again. He is very confident that he can always pick up his course; and he rests by night. That he can fly by night, though, if trained to do so, has now been proved. His home-directing apparatus can tune in by night as well as by day.

The laws that direct a ship's compass never cease either, nor do radio waves, nor the human mind. Whatever the secret of mental telepathic power, it obeys its laws by night and day, irrespective of distance, like the attraction that pulls on the compass needle, like radio waves, like the secret power that directs the pigeon's flight.

One ominous fact has been recorded by pigeon fanciers.

At least, I think it ominous. If a pigeon is released close to a broadcasting station when it is broadcasting, the pigeon's flight seems bewildered. Apparently it finds it difficult to get its bearings, flying hesitantly this way and that, only to wheel and try again. It may be quite a time, and then only after much effort and much circling, before it finally picks lip course and flies away. At times, though, it is so obviously at sea that at last it comes slowly fluttering back to earth. To use a good old Australian term, it is completely bushed.

Now, surely this fact makes us think we are on the right track in surmising that the pigeon really has got some tiny "apparatus" or "receiver" in its little head that can tune into earth waves. If so, then it is easy to understand a pigeon's bewilderment when released close to a working station, for it finds itself in a veritable sea of static. Our pigeon's wave length would be completely jammed, possibly in the same way as wireless stations jam one another during war time.

I wonder now, is it possible? Two thousand million humans are constantly sending out billions of thought waves every hour of the day. The activity of thought is almost certainly mental vibration. The power that works it is almost as certainly some human form of electro-magnetism, just as the earthy form is electric-magnetic waves. If this is so, then the atmosphere must be a sea of waves, of hurrying thought forms. Would one reason why mental telepathy is so difficult to receive be because of the constant interference of these thought waves? Because we have not yet learned how to tune in? The pigeon has been born with his little apparatus already tuned in to whatever power it is that attracts him back to his home loft. He has of necessity used that power daily from babyhood, whereas if we possess it, it has long since atrophied, or gone into slumber through lack of use. We can send at will, can send our thoughts to any person on earth in a second. But as that person is working at his job, with a sea of outside thought waves beating around his head, he does not get our message, naturally. He is tuned in to something else, concentrated on his job, or his daydream, or his worry or pleasure. For he has millions more thoughts rippling through his mind than had his cave man ancestors.

These may seem strange thoughts, but we never learn anything without thought, so here goe!' again:

As a compass needle always points to, is irresistibly attracted to, the north, so the homing pigeon flies to its home, but from any point of the compass. We could say that its home loft is the pigeon's magnetic north. Is the power that directs the pigeon home a live form of the same power that attracts the compass needle irresistibly to the north? Connected with the electro-magnetic waves that have made possible wireless and television? Connected with electrical-chemical-magnetic impulses by which our brain translates into our consciousness the world around us? Without which there would be no You in you, or Me in me? Apparently this same power enables us to think, to receive, and to send out thoughts. This same power helps keep the heart steadily pumping every minute of the day and night, whether the mind is conscious or unconscious.

Dimly now we have become aware of some mighty power all around us and in us. It can be as bulky as the North Pole, or as elusive as a thought in the human mind. It can lie within a lump of iron, or be an invisible "something" in a pigeon's brain.

What is this electro-magnetism that can operate its invisible force. throughout the air, throughout the earth, can guide us by aid of a magnetized needle direct to the north, yet can direct a pigeon to any point of the compass that is home? The thing that can make the air talk, the body of man work and live, the mind of man think and realize?

I believe we have found yet another facet of that which we seek, the directive power within the pigeon's "mind". How and where else does this elusive thing operate among living things? Shall we seek yet another "facet"?

19
WE FIND OUT MORE AND MORE

"I KNOW!" you suggest. "Migratory birds!"

Correct. They possess this directive power also. But they do not use it in such everyday, perfect form, with such all-round control, as the homing pigeon. The migratory birds fly periodically over great distances, returning with change of the seasons; along well-defined routes, from one feeding ground, say, away to a breeding ground, or vice versa; from one climate to another; from one year to the other; from home, away to the "pastures" their parents knew, then back home again.

The mystery Bights of migratory birds are an entrancing study.

Do you know the reasons for these periodic migrations, why the birds purposely endure all that irresistibly undertaken hardship, that terrific, sustained labour? No. Neither do we understand the mechanism and directive power that guide them, bring them back to course even though buffeted for long hours by the fiercest Arctic gales. Though blizzard, icy cold, or breath-taking heat bar the way, they still battle on- and get there, often practically falling to earth after the terrible fatigue of long distances. But they still do it.

Why? and above all-how? Why do our petrels, the shearwaters, periodically leave their hospitable Tasmanian and Victorian homes on the long Bight north to winter on distant shores? They have left a congenial climate, plenty of good food, and even their babies behind them. Within a few weeks the babies take to the air, and follow. What urge is it that impels those babies to leave all the security and comforts of homeland to venture on that long, long trip? But above all, what is it in the babies' heads that guides them to those far-distant shores they have never seen?

So there are two intriguing mysteries for you.

Naturalists believe that the world's greatest flyer is the Arctic tern, which nests in northern Canada and Greenland. This small, slender adventurer with the heart of a thousand lions battles its way across the North Atlantic to Europe, then on down the coast to Africa, and past that continent out on to the Antarctic Ocean. The next spring it flies back. And this is a total distance of 24,000 miles, in distance practically equal to a flight completely around the earth. If Man set out to make a flight around the globe he would require a cumbrous machine that first had to be thought out, invented, built, then serviced: to which he must add fuel, oil, maps, compasses, barometric instruments, pressure instruments, radar, weather detectors, all manner of gadgets. While flying with him would be the uneasy imp suggesting that some of these, or even the whole box of tricks, might break down. But the Arctic tern carries the power in his wee, streamlined little body, and the "know how" guidance in some invisible pin point within his tiny head.

Some animals, and animal herds, migrate yearly, back and forth, as has been known to frontiersmen and naturalists these many years past. Indeed, that birds and beasts possess this directive power was known to the ancients thousands of years ago.

So in migratory birds we have found yet another "facet". It looks more and more as if humans and other living things possess differing forms of this same elusive power. What is it?

Of course, it does not operate under the sea? Yes, it does, in the marvellous migrations of the salmon, of the eels, of many other fishes, of seals! What is this instinctive power that guides millions of hurrying things for thousands of miles through the sea to the one tiny point within some great continent to which they wish to go? I believe it to be the same power, adapted to underwater work. A ship can sail upon the sea, but it can also steam under the sea though it took the human race millions of years to find out how!

Even when Jules Verne dreamed it out but yesterday, they laughed at him. "They" may laugh at you and me, too. But no matter-we are having our own fun trying to think things out.

We may not be so far out either. For numerous things are a form of the same thing, even though they may appear so very different. For instance, take one of the best known, "commonest", things in the world, carbon. Well, charcoal is a form of carbon. Graphite is a stone, but it is a form of carbon. The "writing power" of your lead-pencil is graphite, which is a soft rock, which is charcoal, which is carbon in altered form. The rock graphite is soft, and you know perfectly well how soft charcoal is. You almost certainly know, too, that the diamond is the hardest substance on earth. Well, the diamond is carbon, too.

Compare the cut, glittering, incomparably hard diamond with an ugly-looking old black lump of charcoal that you would crush with your heel. Compare this glittering, more than steel-hard gem with the dull lead in your pencil, so soft it makes a mark on paper. But all of them are the same thing, or, to put it more accurately, perhaps, all are a form of the same thing-carbon. Yet charcoal comes from a living tree which "breathes air" and absorbs sunlight; graphite and the diamond come from the mineralized earth.

Then something else utterly different, ever very close unfortunately, to you and me: pain. You know the difference in earache, in toothache, in belly-ache, in headache. You are fortunately unaware of how many other aches and pains there are. But they are all a form of the very same thing - pain.

Might not this power of the homing pigeon to find its way home, the yearly urge in the "mind" of the great reindeer and other herds, the secret in. the "mind" of migratory birds, the secret in the "mind" of countless millions of migratory fish, be forms of the one power, adapted and developed to the conditions and needs of their own particular environment and life?

And might it not be possible that, smothered by his civilization, an undeveloped form of this same power lies deep within the mind of man? The half guessed at possibilities of mental telepathy, with its allied powers, make one think indeed. And if we understood its laws, might we not be then able to develop and do something worthwhile with it? I'm sure we could.

But let us learn the very little that is known about migratory fish, and what this strange power does to, and for, them.

Fisheries experts and naturalists who have studied the subject of fish migrations tell us that salmon spawn away up in river heads, in fresh water. The baby fish live near where they were born, until two years old; then they swim down river, gradually making their way out into the open sea. They stay away at sea for three years; then they return from the sea, growing into a river of salmon hurrying back to the home river and right up it to the very spot where they were born.

No doubt you have read of the frantic rush of the salmon horde as it battles its way upstream, fighting ever harder against the strength of the rapidly growing current. Presently they are leaping to try to avoid the velocity, leaping when rapids bar their way, too, for nothing must stop them - only death can stop that irresistible urge to reach home.

Now, those fish have spent three years far away out in the open sea. There would be abundance of food there, while life there, especially in the depths and despite enemies, would be much calmer and easier than a long, feverish journey, than a desperate battle against a surging, confined current. What directs their attention, their energies, their entire life force back to land?

You don't know. Neither do I.

What power, instinct, intuition, call it what you like, do those fish possess that guides them from the open sea to their home continent? If a man wishes to travel from, say, France to America, he goes aboard a steamer, because its helm answers to the chartered compass course which directs the vessel there. Or he climbs aboard a plane for the same reason. What would happen to that steamer and plane if they took to sea and air without compass and rudder! But what guides the salmon? What seems to pull it to its distant destination as if by some irresistible magnetic attraction? Not only to land, but to the right continent; not only to the right continent, but to the right *river*.

There are hundreds of river mouths around those thousands of miles of continental coastline. But a fish goes to the right continent, then to the *right* river, the river in which, far up towards its head, it was born. Even when travelling up the river it still knows when not to tum into the wrong stream; it will pass tributary after tributary mouth, creek mouth after creek mouth, until wearily at last it turns aside into the quiet little stream where it was born.

What is the secret that enables the fish to do this? Don't you think it is some form of the same power that guides the migratory bird through space and storms half-way round the world and safely back again? That guides the homing pigeon over foreign lands and right back to its own tiny home?

The story of the eels is even more interesting and puzzling.

Only during recent years, after many centuries of guesswork and wild surmise, have the facts of where the eels migrate to, and what for, and their route back home, been discovered. But the guiding power that takes them where they wish to go, and that brings the babies back home, is still a mystery. The story of our Australian eels I do not know; we have not had the time or the resources to find out. But here are the findings of oversea research men:

The eels live contentedly for years in the ponds and creeks and rivers of North America and Europe. Suddenly there is a slight change of colour and even in internal anatomy amongst them, and they are away, outward bound from ponds and creeks into the rivers, and streaming down to sea. Abandoning the plenteous food in their quiet waters, abandoning safety, too, they head out to sea, chancing vast, unknown waters and the maws of many enemies.

The reason why? And where do they go? And what for? And how do they return? These questions have puzzled man for untold centuries. We know at last that the great swarm from the American coast heads straight to the south-east, while the horde from Europe heads west. From those different -continents both swarms swim straight on far out into the Atlantic Ocean and actually meet at a position which on charts is called the Great Deeps. Down into these mysterious depths the frantic masses of millions of eels slowly sink. Never to come up again! But their children do. It is only in quite recent years that our research men discovered that the clouds of wee things like transparent threads of "nothing" with outsize black eyes that periodically come struggling up from those same Deeps are really baby eels. Untold millions of them, numbers so vast that from the depths they come rising up to the surface like a great, shadowy cloud. And here occurs another miraculous thing. That cloud grows and grows, becomes denser and denser, down in the depths, then upon the surface; then it begins rolling out and spreading and spreading, until finally it separates into two distinct clouds. two vast masses of tiny, baby eels. And now one cloud streams away towards the east, the other heads towards the north-west.

Why does the great cloud separate? Because one cloud wishes to voyage to Europe; the other cloud wishes to go to America! But why do they separate, you ask, or why don't they all go to the same place? Or why don't they separate into many smaller clouds all over the place and go swimming anywhere they like out over the ocean? The Atlantic is big and deep and wide enough surely to goodness - even a fish should know that!

Just so. But the cloud steering east are European eels, and they're determined to go to Europe. While the crowd going westward are American eels and they've got American blood in them - every single one.

"Maybe so," you say doubtfully, "but among all those unknown, millions of tiny things welling up from the Deeps there must be more confusion than in an exploding atom bomb. I'll bet many of those American eels get mixed up with the others and are sailing to Europe at this moment! I bet many of those European babies are now busily emigrating to America."

Not so, my friend. Every American eel is an American type, while every European is a European type; and each and every single one will reach its correct destination.

"Well, if they're only just born, and so tiny, and so indistinguishably alike, how do they know one from the other?"

"Ask me! I don't know!"

"Well then, how do the American eels know how to head for America, and the European for Europe?"

"I don't know that, either. If you can tell me what that sense of urge and of direction is, and how it works in the homing pigeon's head, then I believe you'll have the answer."

However, that is what happens. The American eels reach America, the European reach Europe. But, unlike their parents, hurrying away, they take their time. They dawdle along while feeding for two or three years until, on reaching land, they have grown into the familiarly known elver. And now here another wonderful thing happens. For every elver seeks out the very river mouth from which his parents put to sea; and he swims straight on up that river, on and on, wriggling on and up against the foaming fury of rapids, even climbing, wriggiing up waterfalls until at last he glides into the quiet pool from which his parents came.

"Why do they do it?" you wonder. To me, "*How* do they find their way there?" is the greater wonder. An eel, born in vasty deeps, finds its way across thousand of miles of ocean to a land it has never seen, to a river mouth it has never known, then right away up to a creek it has never known, to a pool it has never known. What is the power within the eel that irresistibly guides it to that one wee spot over all that distance, against all those fantastically strange conditions?

You and I could yarn for a long time about such fascinating mysteries of life, mysteries only because we have not yet been clever enough to find out the reasons why. Once we do discover these things our strange facts will be no longer mysteries, for we will find them regulated by iron-bound laws of nature: as everything is, upon and under the earth, the sea, the atmosphere, the universe. Everything, literally everything, does what it does because of guiding laws created by the Great Engineer. We merely have not yet found out the laws that awaken, develop, and govern the secret direction born into certain birds, fishes, animals, and the mysteries lying mostly dormant within the human mind.

Don't you now believe that all these particular mysteries in birds, fishes, animals, and man are facets of the one diamond? That each stems from the same power, regulated to carry out its special job according to the conditions of life and environment of the particular living thing? Probably, too, the ever-active magnetism of the earth and atmospheric air are a form of that very same power.

What if we try to discover a "something" that appears to drive this "power" into action? When the homing pigeon is liberated its whole being, on feeling its wings, is concentrated on the wish to be "home". This concentrated wish, this strong emotion, seems to be the "trigger" which not only sets its guidance power working, but also supplies greatly increased strength and endurance to the body. The wish is father of the thought, as it were. And it almost certainly is some thought power, some particular mental power, which gives the guidance.

With the migratory bird, it is some attraction in the particular season that sets it longing to go somewhere, to the exclusion of all else. Here again this concentrated wish appears to be the motive - power that sets its guidance "ticking" to direct and give physical power to its body to take it to just where it longs to go.

The same with the salmon, the same with the eels. They get that concentrated urge, that frantic wish to be in some very particular place even thousands of miles away. And this emotion wakes up the "direction finder" in their heads and guides them there, also giving them greater physical power of speed and endurance to enable the body to battle on its way.

This elusive "mental ghost" exerts a perfectly accurate directive, and has a tremendously powerful effect upon the body. In exact direction and for a long time continued duration, it moves flesh and bone, muscle and nerve and sinew in living things - some of which are far more powerful and weightier than you and me. The reindeer and buffalo, the walrus and seal; then birds and fishes. And remember, flesh is flesh and bone is bone, whether in humans or animals. And a happy feeling is a happy feeling, and pain is pain. Remember, too, that this elusive thing that moves the body so strenuously is always correct; it always does the right thing, and for the good of the body.

Is there some form of this same power in man? I believe there is. And the key to this particular power may be in that compartment of the mind devoted to such elusive activities as mental telepathy and hypnotism, which are apparently closely related to the subconscious mind. It seems to me that the same laws that work these mysteries among certain birds, fishes, and animals, work telepathy and hypnotism in the human mind. With the birds, fishes, and animals the "power" is already "connected". Could we connect this power, which is almost certainly within us, connect it to the conscious mind when it was needed for the body's good?

Don't forget that medical science has discovered that the subconscious mind works for the body every second of the night and day, ever battling to keep it in working order. And this practically unknown servant of ours does a marvellously good job for us when some "wrongness" enters into us, works steadily, then frantically, to overwhelm the might-be fatal intruder and drive it out-while all the time our physical body can only lie there waiting, perhaps in misery and in pain.

If circumstances were dead against the subconscious and its work was slowly being stifled and beaten, what a mighty aid it would be if we were able *consciously* to call this mental power to help the sub-conscious! Remember the miraculous *rightness* of direction this power gives to the living things we have been discussing; remember the *super* strength and endurance it infuses into those physical bodies as they battle through storm and icy blizzards, or over great areas of land, or through thousands of miles of ocean - everything concentrated on forcing those bodies to do the right thing and thus attain the right end. Our end would be the end of pain, then the regaining of perfect bodily health: by connecting, through the conscious mind, this power within to aid the sub-conscious in its fight for health.

If this were possible - if the You in you, and the Me in me knew how to call up this powerful body-urger to marshall its reserves what a heaven-sent position humanity would be in to control its own health!

Well, our yarning time is up. If we understood the unknown powers within our minds we should know the meaning of the world and the universe.

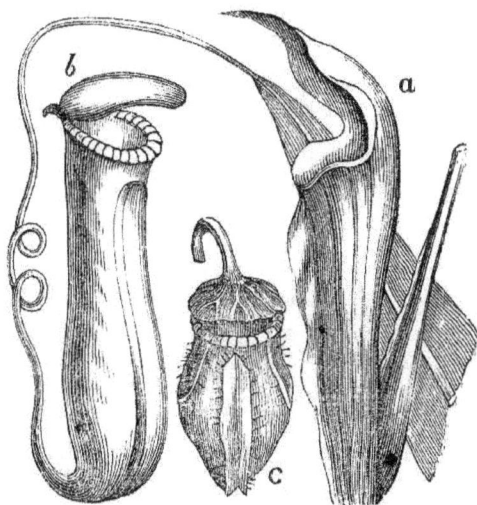

The carnoverous Pitcher Plant.

20

A STORY OF THE SWAMPS:
CUPS OF DEATH

HAVE you ever thought about swamps? Dismal things, filled with the croak of frogs; mud, and wretchedness by night; chill breath from water-soaked reeds, wail of the curlew.

But there are swamps and swamps. Some are lovely; others are intriguing with their numerous forms of life and their mysterious depths. Others again are just swamps; and the inner hearts of the great ones can be terrifying. Dangers may lurk in that gloomy loneliness: partly submerged masses of tendrils and vines and water-plants, as deadly as the slimy arms of countless octopuses; untold depths of mud, sticky glue that, once it grips a struggling thing, silently sucks down-down-down. Danger, too, from the fangs of the water-snake, from the crocodile. That hideous brute, at home in the primal mud, is a lurking menace in some of the large coastal swamps.

Yet swamps can be very beautiful, the gorgeous flowers of water lilies playing with the sunlight, the air elusively scented, alive with the happy calls of birds, the clear bottom a fairy mosaic of coloured pebbles and sands over which swim fat, moon-eyed fish. In isolated places water maids may be playing there, too; and, from cover of the lovely trees, you will hear girlish voices in merry laughter. Peer from the tree trunks and you will see, rising from the clear water, a laughing maid holding high a wriggling tortoise, the sun glinting bronze upon her chocolate tinted skin. Another rises beside her, then another and another. They gasp and blow and snort in imitation of an old man dugong, their big dark eyes sparkling in delight. For a wealth of foodstuffs, vegetable and fish and bird, also abound in such pleasant waters.

Some swamps are noisy with life, a perfect bedlam of waterfowl, of scrub, forest, and jungle bird life; the reed-clustered shores full of mysterious rustlings, then loud with the rooting, the grunting, of the wild pig, the soft "Thud! thud! thud!" of the swamp wallaby. Other swamps are quiet and still, their various tinted waters and vegetation and islets and reed cluttered banks hiding a life of their own; mysterious indeed.

Perhaps some of the strangest swamps are the Pitcher Plant swamps of Cape York Peninsula. These very small swamps were, to me, most fascinating. One in particular (that had me crawling about on hands and knees, experimenting for hours at a time with unfortunate Hies and other insects) is situated in that awful turkey-bush scrub near the mouth of the Escape River - a weird place. Kennedy, the explorer, was speared just there, the end of his goal in sight, his comrades in misery perishing far behind.

This particular little swamp is crowded with hungry, clever plants that eat meat. Really so, for though the "meat" is only the flies so plentiful in the bush, the bees and ants, the beetles and butterflies and insects, still it is meat all the same. These plants are called Pitcher plants, perhaps because their "Bower", which seems to me the plant itself, grows in the shape of an old-time pitcher, the large clay vase that Rachael carried to the well. Other varieties of meat-eating plants in other localities, however, are sometimes shaped differently. Our cunning meat-eater grows in sizes from that of a thimble up to that of a large vase: this vase part of the plant appears to be actually the Bower, and it is veritably a Bower of death. It is a green, or yellowish-green, or reddish-green leaf, shaped much like a wide-mouthed tumbler. If you gaze down into this "tumbler" its beautifully smooth sides (inside) appear ever so inviting, clean and cool; now that clean, yellowish looking bottom of the tumbler is surely moving, like a woman gently breathing in sleep; and now it is slowly opening out, and there comes gently welling up into the cup a clear liquid, until the bottom is a quarter-inch full. Gently the bottom closes, the liquid is quiescent, sparkling-what a tempting sip to any thirsty little thing! Before our nose, now, the rim of the cup is swelling outward; then slowly it grows still. This cup of death is open to the wide blue sky, inviting some passing victim to partake of the nectar deep within.

A native bee flies overhead, banks on a sharp turn as he flies downward toward the cup. He hesitates, hovers a moment, then flies down and alights on the rim of the cup. He peers downward, begins to crawl down the inside of the cup towards the nectar; he seems to be sliding, as if that beautifully smooth downward surface were coated with a film of oil. Now the bee seems to be slipping - and he slips straight down into the nectar. Agitatedly he bobs up, struggles back to the side of the cup, attempts to take off and fly up. His wings are clogged; he falls back into the nectar. He flounders again to the side of the cup, laboriously crawls up his own length, begins to clean his wings. He appears to experience some further difficulty, slips back into the nectar again. Wretchedly now he struggles to the side of the cup, and begins to climb again.

Heavily burdened with his water-logged wings, his tiny feet all sticky, what a height upward to the free blue sky the smooth wall of that cup must now appear to our little bee; and what a struggle commences as, in clogged bewilderment, he seeks escape from this fearsome prison. Desperately he manages to struggle an inch, then another inch, up this prison wall. He clings there; we see he is gasping for breath and strength; slowly he begins to struggle up again.

And now something awful is happening down there before our startled eyes. From the smooth bowl of the plant there grope out a myriad of the tiniest spikes, an array of needle-like lances, pointing downward. As the bee comes up to them his head rises, sways this way and that, as he seeks a way over the massed lances threatening his chest. But there is no way over. No matter which way he wriggles, turns, squirms, there is always a lance pointing at his throat. He loses his head, frantically now tries to climb up and over; he slips, or loses balance, or is pushed and falls right back down again into the nectar.

It is a frightened bee that struggles upright, that now crawls slowly back to the side of the cup, clings for breath, wearily attempts to shake the cloying stuff from his sogged wings, then begins that climb all over again. And we who are watching him over the open cup can imagine how his tiny heart must now be bursting from labour and fear. Slowly, slowly he reaches that array of spears again; and yet again he falls, or is pushed back.

And so that terrible, that hopeless struggle will commence all over again until he falls back for the last time - to drown helplessly in the nectar that he had believed was food of life.

But what is death to the insect means life to the plant. And the struggle for survival must surely be grim for the plant, too, at times. For despite the breeding-grounds in the tangled vegetation, the wind-swept grasses and the queer river near by, there must surely be a famine of insects at times. Some, if not all, of these plants are voracious things. Here is one whose death-trap is thick with bogged and drowning insects, its nectar now clogged with their little black and brown, red and grey, white and russet, bodies. As we gaze down into that bogged helplessness, a slow movement seems to be, yes, is growing within the very plant. Slowly the wide open rim of the deep cup is closing in upon itself! Slowly the cup seems to be shrinking down into itself! It appears then as if the bowl were dividing into tightly clenched petals bending in towards, then growing into, one another, like the fingers of a slowly clenching hand. The cup has now quite closed over and slowly is shrinking down into itself: and you wonder what quiet, grim muscular opening and closing is taking place deep down within, where the insects are. Are they being sucked down into what--? Are they being absorbed? The bowl now is no larger than a tennis ball, is squeezing yet tighter within itself until it lies quiescent upon the ground. Surely it is sleeping now!

Definitely not. Not just yet, anyway. We cannot see the mystery within, but we know. The plant is eating, hungrily enjoying its meal; soon it will be digesting it, just as you digest meat and food. For that nectar is changing to digestive juices, now this carnivorous plant is digesting its meat. Is it actually a living stomach? It is difficult to imagine a flower being a living stomach.

We notice now that there are numerous other plants that we thought were but curled up leaves upon the ground - all plants digesting their meal. Countless others everywhere stand erect with their cups wide open to the sky. What do they feel? Do they feel anything as a butterfly in its delicate beauty comes hovering; are they straining in invitation, doing their utmost to coax the prey to flutter down for its sip of death? What silent rivalry there must be amongst all those plants, what unknown powers have they in striving to add yet further lure to excite the senses of insects? Perhaps a stronger waft of scent to their nectar, a sweeter perfume to the deadly smooth bowl of their cup, perhaps a something we cannot guess at as added attraction upon the wide open rim.

As we bend down to gaze more closely, that vegetable ball right under our nose is moving, swelling! Is slowly swelling more, and slowly coming upright, growing into the shape of a cup as its thick petals now begin to bulge upward, outward, then unfold. Yes, it really is a cup taking shape, as the petals unfold outward and upright. This cup seems only half grown. There is no nectar down there now; the yellowish glossiness of the bottom is covered with husks, pathetic husks of wings, of tiny limbs, of wee heads, the sucked-out husks of little victims. Alas! the very heart of our flower is a cesspool of corpses; all else is gone into the life of the plant. These remnants are the veriest glimpses of skeletons, fragile as a breath. Yet we recognize what was once the wings of a beetle, the legs of a grasshopper, the crumpled up, faded, blue and purple wings of a butterfly.

The plant cannot digest these hard things, as we cannot digest bones. But now down in the cup the bottom is gently rising up, as the petals fold down outside and around it. And then, almost imperceptibly, with the slightest pulsing movement, the plant has thrown out, has ejected, its refuse.

Slowly the bottom sinks down within itself, and now the petals unfold upward, growing again into the form of a cup. The sides take their nice clean shape as the cup stretches upward and the rim stretches up and out, full open. Deep down in the cup there is a slight movement, and out come the first glistening drops of nectar.

Slowly it wells up into the bottom of the cup, so clean and clear and inviting, and becomes quiescent.

We can almost feel the plant breathing, as under the warm sunshine it patiently awaits its new first victim, its appetite slowly growing.

Over the wide bushland comes scent of flowering tree with tang of water plants. A cockatoo screeches away up over the rise, a fish plops in the river. There comes the important hum of a big March fly, a bee alights on. a flower, the still air seems alive with hum, with buzz of busy insects.

Flowers are closing, flowers are digesting, flowers are slowly opening their cups of death.

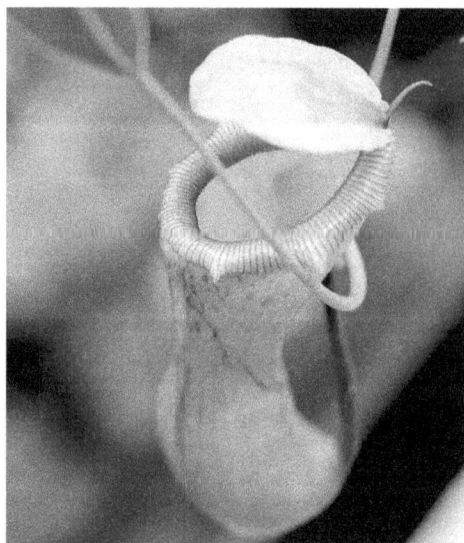

21
COME "SWAMPING" WITH ME

SOME swamps are dismal holes; others, rich in vegetable and water life, are prolific. breeding-grounds for varieties of waterfowl, many of which you've never heard of, for bush birds that inhabit the fringes, because such swamps supply plentiful food. Then there are the swamp wallaby, the smaller marsupials, the droves of wild pigs, and often, too, the dingo and the fox. Snakes and lizards, both land and water, frequent swamps, and furry water-rats that vanish in a Bash. There are fish, and sometimes eels, tortoise and crayfish. And in the far northern swamps the long-homed, slate-grey buffalo, the hideous, heavy-jowled crocodile.

Where the buffalo herds, led by the bulls, go strolling out on to the plains with the dawn, wild cattle and ponies can be met in the swamps; and wild turkey, doves cooing around the bamboo jungles, quaint spoonbills, squatter pigeons that Butter through the trellised maze of the strange banyan-trees. Quite possibly you will spy upon a bower-bird's nest while the shy host is busy making love. Always you will hear the hoarse poo-hoo-hoo! of the swamp pheasant; and, if out in the wild places, you may see a canoe come gliding out of a creek, the dark-skinned paddlers happy that their little craft is loaded with duck and geese eggs.

And of course you'll meet old Jabaroo, the giant stork, who, with his great long legs and beak, looks quite capable of sailing through the skies with a baby in his beak. That big solemn old fellow, if seen on a bright day between some queer reflection of still water and sunlight, grows to mirage height, even as tall as the branches of trees. I've never forgotten my astonishment at one such optical illusion, for the monstrous bird towered right up to the branches while his gigantic, grotesque reflection waS thrown far away out over the still, gleaming water.

In such swamps, the big ones that merge away back into the foothills, the noise of a pleasant day may rise to bedlam. The swift whirr and splash of arriving ducks, the cluckings and whistlings of myriads away out on the swamp, the honk of geese, the harsh cackling of waterhens feeding among the reeds, the splashing of pelicans, trumpet calls of brolgas dancing along the banks, the hoarse boom of some big old crane, whistling of parrots, screeching of flocks of cockatoos and galahs, kark of crows, the whistling and cooing and trilling of innumerable smaller birds: it is a fascinating medley of vivid life. If something disturbs this teeming life, a man's shout would be lost in the deafening tumult as flock after flock of duck, geese, pelican, crane, churn up from the water, and as thousands upon thousands of land birds rise, with deafening screeches from flocks of cockatoo, galah and parrot. The beating of those countless wings is a rumble in the sky, now filled with a tornado of screeching, whistling, cackling, honking, above a softly falling rain of coloured feathers.

There is another form of swamp where life is much quieter, where silence and stealth seem the rule of life. Such places are gloomy with their scrubby patches of trees, their cluttered bush and vine, their little islets covered with coarse grasses. Instead of being a sparkling sheet of clear water, this swamp is mostly of channels of still water, part choked with reeds and vine among motionless clumps of trees. And treacherous the soggy earth may be: a man stepping from tussock to tussock could easily make a false step here and find himself sinking to the waist in sticky mud. And that is a terrible feeling, with the only thing to grasp a tussock that comes away in your clutching hands. And yet suddenly, in the very heart of such a dismal place, you may come upon something very beautiful. Surrounded by the dull grey or dark green of stunted trees, a sheet of the snowiest white, all aglint from the sun high in the clear blue sky: An egret colony. The islet one snow-white mass from the beautifully feathered birds. Happily, there are no egret hunters here to slaughter the serenity of this lovely sight.

A different sort of swamp again is an arm of the sea, where the tide comes creeping in along the shallow creeks and depressions, and still on, trickling among and past the shore trees to creep out over the grasslands. Listen! and you can hear it softly murmuring as it comes. See its millions of rivulets creeping on, only to die down, to reappear, coming in a little greater force to surge and spread yet a little farther on. To die again, then come creeping again, a little faster, a little stronger, travelling a little farther - like twisting snakes, presently running one into the other to form a tiny pool which even as you watch steadily grows, spreads, and then pool joins pool while new rivulets go creeping on ahead. Soon you hear it hissing as suddenly the earth is covered an inch deep with water. Soon you must move farther back. It can creep thus over miles of country where the shore is sufficiently lowlying. Then it is creeping out into the bushland grasses. And very soon, where there were acres of grasses and bushes, you suddenly see the sheen of the sun upon water, still creeping farther out into the bushland, spreading, spreading, growing deeper, stronger. There is mighty power behind that quiet, creeping menace.

When big tides come thus and swamp the grasslands there generally come also many hungry fish of all sizes. For countless grasshoppers and beetles, spiders and things of the grasses and bushes will have been surprised by the submerging, encircling waters, with here and there a startled snake scurrying from the bath of his life. Rich food these trapped ones are to the fishes that get busy while the going is good. And so, too, do the cranes and hawks. For here and there a fish in the new shallows, hampered by the grasses and bushes, falls a prey to talon and beak.

A real mangrove swamp is a gloomy place. The gnarled roots of the mangrove stick up out of mud and water to half the height of a man, ugly and crooked and twisted, like most things of the mud, stretching away in the gloom like millions of writhing snakes suddenly petrified. The dull, monotonous grey-green of the mangroves grows so thickly that all below is gloom. No grasses here, just grey or blue mud-though if such a swamp is on a coral shore then strangely enough the little pools where creeks come gurgling in with the tide are sometimes lined with pure white coral sand. These pools are so transparent as to make the depth of water surprisingly deceptive. There is space among the trees around such pools, and here sunlight pours straight down and tinges the gloom with gold. Everywhere a damp smell of mud, an uncanny silence. Then, dulled by branches and leaves a "Plop!" The fall of a mangrove pod. And this occasional muffled "Plop! Plop! Plop!" goes on day and night.

You think there could not possibly be life in such a wretched place. But a "Hiss!" at your feet and a small hole opens in the mud; it half closes, then opens to a "Hiss!" while up from it comes a wee bubble that slowly grows and expands with a slimy iridescence. It hovers there, seemingly clinging desperately to the mud rim, then bursts and collapses with a sigh like a dying fairy. But the rim of the little hole now stays put; the bubble laboriously forced up through the mud has in some way lined that pencil-like shaft.

Something is alive away down there in that gluey mess, maybe some weird shellfish, busily engaged in mining for-what? In curiosity you peer right down at the hole, only to withdraw your head distastefully as to your offended nostrils comes the faint odour of some stinking gas. What manner of a thing is it that works and lives and does its business in beastly mud, that is not only a miner in material that taxes all inventions of the civilized engineer to defy, but can also call upon the gases of mud and decaying vegetation and fish offal to help it!

Suddenly you become aware that you are an object of considerable interest. You were curious about the invisible miner deep down in the mud; but you, too, are an object of curiosity in this gloomy element. Numbers of eyes, goggle-eyed, stupid-looking, but comically friendly, are gazing up at you from the mangrove roots at your feet, from the roots across the pool, too. Quaint little browney-grey fishes of some sort with piggish, absurdly large heads on rounded, tapering bodies. Then you see others, half hopping, half flapping across the mud towards you. You suddenly wonder that Goggle-eyes is right out of the water, apparently suffering no inconvenience at all. Others of the creatures are climbing right up out of the water on to the mangrove roots; and the stupid-looking heads of others are leering up at you from holes in the mud.

This, then, is how they survive: When the tide comes creeping in, and with it the hungry fish, these wise little humorists pop down into their burrows, built so deep that the snouting nose of a fish, the rooting claws of a crab, cannot dig them out; and they wait there, perhaps sleep in peace, until at last the tide recedes and they come popping out into their own again.

You wonder how these quaint things breathe out of the water.

They seem quite at home in the air, as in the water. You notice that most are lying up on a mangrove root, with only their tails in the water. And that is how they breathe in oxygen from the water, so some naturalists believe-through their tails.

The white of a large shell takes your eye; it is twice the size of your clenched hand. But it is moving, slowly, leaving a fresh, plain track behind it in the mud. Then you see some weird looking thing that really is dragging it along. Down through the water it looks repulsive, something like the head and fleshy neck of a gigantic spider, apparently with great hairy legs reaching slowly out, dragging the large shell. You throw a stick: at the splash, the fleshy thing instantly withdraws; only the shell is lying quietly on the bottom as the ripples fold away. You see then that there are smaller shellfish in the pool, and you realize that those long lines, as if the point of a stick had been gently dragged across the bottom of the pool, are really the tracks of shellfish.

Other things than shellfish live glued to mangrove roots. Some even make cement tubes up along the roots, and within these sheltering tunnels live and love and rear families and die. Clever workers these must be, to know how to select and mine and mix their materials from the stuff of the mud and lime from coral sands. You realize there are many more holes, shafts, in fact countless tunnels in and under these acres of mud. What great numbers of things there must be living down there, and what great labour must ceaselessly be going on! Labour not only in seeking things to eat, but in constant building. For the weight of the tide must surely close up millions of holes; and then they must be cleaned out, bored out, or blown out again. It is quite possible though, and very probable, that many of the tunnels are lined with materials that defy weight and pressure both of mud and water.

Somewhat irritably, you flick the back of your neck. Sitting on the roots of the old mangrove-tree you've done it before: a few grains of dust seem occasionally to fall upon your neck as you gaze into the pool. You know that is unlikely, for through this dense roof of uncountable leaves dust could not penetrate. Half thinking about it you lean your cheek back against the trunk and become aware of a tiny sound, as of something boring. Yes, with your ear to the trunk, you can imagine some industrious worker with a hard, sharp tool, a veritable augur, boring steadily into wood. And so it is. As you look up a wee puff of powder shoots out of the trunk and falls fair in your eye.

That is it - sawdust! Kicked out by the energetic worker above.

You stand up, put your ear to the fresh, tiny hole, and very distinctly now you can hear him working, working hard. By the sound you can almost see the working of his marvellously tempered, sharp-cutting tool, almost feel him putting his weight into it as he bores steadily on, on, on into the very heart of the tree.

How much life there is in this vast pit of apparently lifeless desolation! Life everywhere in the mud, life everywhere in this gloomy labyrinth of silent trees. If we could magnify the life sounds, the work sounds, the love sounds, the fight sounds, the death sounds, of these millions of strugglers in mud and timber, what an unimaginable roar of sound it would be!

We lean back from the tree and listen.

An eerie quietness, a shuddersome loneliness. And then, the soft burst of some gas bubble, the soft, distinct "Plop!" away out there somewhere.

22

MYSTERIES OF THE MANGROVES

STEPPING from root to root, you leave this pool, a hand to the trunks, because many a curved root is treacherous and will snap beneath your weight. The branches of the gnarled trunks grow so close together their leaves blot out the sunlight. You are about to step down on to a mud patch when your foot draws swiftly back to a "Clash!" and you glare down at the upraised, threatening claws of a huge crab, each claw the size of your clenched fist, the pincers powerful enough to chew into coral. What a mess they would have made of your bare, soft foot! The body of the thing is as large as a dinner-plate, coloured dull bluish-purple; you would never have seen it on the mud but for the clash of those threatening claws.

Similar crabs, out by the edge of the swamp, dig burrows for themselves in the coral, just as rabbits dig burrows. As the tide sighs out, they emerge and ravish the pools for small fish, or dead things, or any living thing they can seize and devour. As the tide comes gurgling in they return close to their burrows, awaiting prey, but ready with startling speed to dive down into their dugouts if a big fish comes speeding at them.

You come to another pool, a long pool left in a depression when the tide had gurgled away back to sea. You wonder at the crystal clearness of this pool; you can see every grain of sand upon the bottom. Gazing down from the roots you see it is empty of life, and you think you will step down and walk along its clear, inviting water path. A "something", a consciousness of movement, halts you even before the eye distinguishes the array of ghastly teeth arming the fiendish jaws slowly swaying from side to side. You are gazing straight down into the open mouth of a monstrous eel, its snake-like head and mouth protruding from its burrow in the mud. They are awful things, their rows of needle-pointed teeth a terror, their thick, slimy bodies a twisting, writhing mass of muscle when they fasten upon a large prey.

You've received quite a shock, staring down at that horrid thing with its glistening snake-like eyes glaring straight up at you. You reach up, break off a small mangrove branch and jab down at the horrid thing. Instantly the stick is torn from your hand as in a flurry of mud the head withdraws into the burrow. But as the water slowly clears there is the head again, slowly swaying, open-mouthed, teeth gleaming.

There are many such brutes, of all sizes, lurking throughout this mangrove forest. But the commotion with that stick has disturbed the water and you are surprised to see a goodly sized fish dart across the pool and vanish. You step across the slippery roots away from the eel, break another branch and thrash the water. Fish dart from everywhere, instantly to vanish. You are amazed, for you had seen no sign of a fish; and as the water slowly quietens you see no further sign. Yet the water is crystal clear, and in its very deepest part barely two feet deep, hardly that.

It takes experience to see fish in such a pool. Such a tiny pool, yet there may well be a hundred fish of all sizes in it. They are sheltering in, under and between the maze of mangrove roots fringing the pool. You stare straight down under your feet. The water here is barely a foot deep, and dear as crystal. Not the faintest sign of a fish, only the intertwined roots, with a small leaf caught between them, very slowly moving from some faint water movement. But that "leaf" is the fin of a fish and his bright eyes are staring straight up at you. His body is leaning against a root; root and body are exactly the same greenish-grey colour.

You step on over the roots and come to a long, narrow pool barely one foot deep. Its crystal-clear bottom looks inviting to walk upon. Making sure there is no wicked head of an eel swaying from a burrow you step down and walk along the pool, and pleasant it is after that crouching, stepping walk from root to root. You are sorry when you reach the end of the pool, again terraced by roots. As you step up to climb out your foot is heaved up as by an earthquake and you are thrown Hat back with a mighty splash. The pool is lashed into waves as you struggle up and spring fearfully for the roots-you could not have stepped upon anything less than a crocodile! You are away up on the roots clinging to the branches before you gaze behind, trying to pull your heart back down your throat. The shallow pool is all waves, lapping at the roots. Another mighty splash and you see it-a monstrous rock cod! There he is in the shallows wedged now against the roots, his huge head, glaring eyes, leathery lips apparently gibbering at you. As your fright gradually subsides with the wavelets you are astounded at the size of this mighty fish in this so shallow pool - he must weigh fully as much as you do.

I have seen truly enormous fish in such pools. Full-bellied when the tide goes out, they simply laze there until the tide shall come surging in to take them back to the sea again.

You are surprised and startled by now to realize that this gloomy, apparently lifeless labyrinth is alive with mystifying creatures of all sorts and sizes; and you creep on over the roots again, anxious lest you be caught by some unexpected terror when the tide comes in. The gloom through the trunks gradually lightens until you are pleasantly surprised at clear daylight amongst the countless branches. With a sigh of relief, you step out into open, glorious sunlight, a carpet of purest blue above.

This, now, is the tiniest of "lakes", a clear pool densely hemmed in by the branches and trunks and roots of much taller mangroves. Cranes of varying sizes around the lake stand and stare at you, others peer down from the branches above the pool. White cranes and blue, and little water birds on long, stilt-like legs. They are all silent, and solemn-solemnity and silence fit this place. You glance up at the sky in surprise at a cloud scudding fast overhead. Far away out in the open world a strong wind is blowing. But no breath of it penetrates this impenetrable maze of trees, trunks, branches, roots. The birds still stare-you are a truly remarkable sight to them. You wonder that none of them are fishing - but then, what could they catch here? Yet all these silent birds are plump, for there is plenty to eat here.

Down in the crystal water a tiny whiff of "smoke" forms, spreads, comes floating up as a wee cloud. It is the finest of sediment stirred up by the nose of a fish rooting into the bottom for shellfish. The cloud is suddenly joined by a flurry of sand as the fish shoots ahead, and now you see the flat "wings", long, whip-like tail, of a stingray. Idly he surfaces, slowly turns round, and you see his little eyes peering across at you, his blue wings quiescent on the surface like the floating leaves of a water-lily.

You throw a stick at him and immediately the pool becomes alive with stingrays, from babies the size of a plate, to a monster whose "wings" are five feet across. Slate-grey rays, blue rays, black rays, heaving up from the bottom to cruise the surface at this splash which has shattered their peace. Some of the cranes fly with a hoarse, trumpet-like cry to alight heavily. on the branches overhead. A young sawfish, disturbed by the stingrays, shoots across the tiny lake in a lather of foam, fish leaping aside from that cruel weapon of his. As you watch there comes to your ears a low murmuring, from far away. You turn back to the roots intent on making your way back, away from this tangled morass. For that low murmur is not a sighing of a breeze over the tree-tops; it is the first breath of the incoming tide. Soon, that murmuring will grow into a whispering, a rustling, then a hissing, a rapidly oncoming gurgling. Soon it will grow into a mighty coughing as the water surges in ever deeper and faster in a frenzied rush over the roots.

By nightfall the water will be surging six and seven feet deep over the roots, possibly right up to the lower branches of the mangroves. And with it will come countless hungry fish of all sizes. What thrashings of the water, what struggles then and frenzied escapes, as they chase prey amongst this vast maze of roots and tree-trunks. A terrifying experience for a man to be trapped there then, clinging up amongst those slender branches all night, seeing nothing but splashes of water, churned, phosphorescent, but hearing the hissings and splashings, the thumps of struggling bodies against the tree-trunks at his feet, the clashing of teeth, frightening noises splashing up from the enveloping water mystery in the black night.

I was trapped once like that and never want the experience again.

23

THE CUIRASS

THOUGH anyone with the eyes to see would find something of interest in any Australian swamp, even the most fascinating of our northern swamps are as nothing compared to the vast swamps of New Guinea. In the Fly River area in western Papua, and in the Sepik River area in the Mandated Territory the great swamp lands could almost be classed as inland seas: Seas in which gleam lovely blue lakes, and frightful morasses; in which there are swamps within swamps, and thousands of square miles of giant water grasses; in which there are jungles, and vast labyrinths of mud and water and unbelievable mazes of overpowering vegetation. Though some hundreds of miles apart, both great swamp systems are fed by these two mighty rivers and their tributaries: Western Papua by the Fly, the Mandated Territory by the Sepik. The estuary of the Fly is forty miles across; the waters of the Sepik inland in flood can stretch fifty miles wide. A vast bar blocks the mouth of the Fly and it can be navigated only by launch, for some five hundred miles inland; but the Sepik can be navigated by small steamer for four hundred and fifty miles. Along both rivers, here and there, are chains of islands; and each has its floating islands also. The vast mass of water that churns down these rivers daily gouges out enormous blocks of the banks from higher upstream, and sends them slowly on their way as real floating islands, held together by their trees and vegetation and the mat-work of intertwined roots. Slowly a mighty, irresistible mass comes floating downstream and all craft must give way to it. If it reaches the river mouth without being slowly turned back by the tide (the Fly, for instance, is tidal for some 200 miles), it is gradually pounded and rocked to pieces by the waves; but sometimes a backwash gradually pushes it back against the river banks. Like a live thing its hawsers of roots reach out into the mud of the bank and begin to grow, while roots and vegetation from the bank reach out for and into it. And in a surprisingly short time the bank has claimed its own again; the island is anchored and soon becomes once more portion of the mother river-bank. In yet another way Nature's engineering snatches back what would otherwise be waste of precious land. There comes a bend in the river where current or backwash carries one, or even two, floating islands back on to the shallows where they are grounded until the next big flood; but before then the channel between the bank and island, and between the islands themselves, begins to silt up, then the silting becomes more rapid, cementing island to bank and island to island. Watergrass springs up in the accumulating silt, thus binding it, and further binding island to island. Vegetation begins creeping out over the silting channels, making them silt more quickly - until in triumph once again the river-bank has reclaimed its breakaway prodigal.

From the great mountain chain running through Dutch New Guinea other rivers and countless streams come pouring down to merge with these two great rivers. And it rains heavily up there practically every day in the year. So perhaps you can hazily imagine the sea of water regularly pouring down to swell the great rivers and seep far away out over the low-lying lands. This forms the great swamps, so vast that they carry their own lakes and floating islands. There is very little animal life in those thousands of square miles of swamps, but there are untold varieties of fish life, of bird life - and unfortunately there are crocodiles, too. Some of the most beautiful birds in the whole world (Birds of Paradise, for instance, and marvellous pigeons) live their life of joy and sorrow along those great rivers and swamps. Waterfowl life, in those regions suitable to it, is almost unbelievable in it prodigality.

In the areas of these great swamp lands, from the river's edge away back to coast or mountains, live many native tribes of varying degrees of culture: from the animal-like swamp savages who flit past like wraiths and are gone, to the highly cultured river men, fine builders of great houses and mighty canoes, wonderful carvers, agriculturists, singers and dancers.

Among the swamp lands of both great river systems there lie swamps within swamps, and probably the most useful of these to man are the "sac-sac" swamps - in our language, the sago palm swamps. A sac-sac swamp, gloomy and quiet, its gaunt palms like motionless sentinels, its trees gnarled and scabby-trunked, strange-looking fronds drooping over stagnant mud. Huge logs lie in weed-covered slime, their long rotted bark eaten into by green and brown and grey fungus and mosses. Slow bubbles well up out of the mud; water pools are black, some quite inky-black, where fallen sago trunks lie gutted, their rusty pith decaying in the sludge, turning the air sour. Grey-green cables, motionless, like knotted hawsers trellised with vines, loop down from nameless palms. Curtains of russet-grey creepers droop from gnarled branches like shrouds in some dying primeval forest. Bunches of clustered vines, devoid of all movement, drape dead trees as they die with them. Stealthy sighs, whisperings, croaks from mud hidden under a blanket of peeled-off bark and decaying leaves. A swamp like this seems a whisper from the past of the life of primeval ages.

Though some of the sac-sac swamps are very gloomy places, the sago palm itself is truly a tree of life. If you were wandering towards one you'd probably hear the sound of chopping, the laughter of children, the chatter of gossiping women - that is, if they believed they were safe from the prying eyes of friend or foe. These little brown women with their great mops of fuzzy hair, clad in their short grass skirts, are more or less industriously chopping into the trunks of the sac-sac palms to adze out the pith preparatory to preparing it for the making of sago. Not an easy job, for the bark of the sago palm is covered with long, sharp thorns. It needs practice and strong hands to strip that tough bark, then chop into the tougher trunk, then chop out the hard, stringy white pith, then beat it into a soft consistency. But unless the men are hungrily waiting away back in the village the women will make a pleasure of the work in gossip, joke, and laughter. By and by, as the process goes on to completion, they will pack large bundles of sago rolls to a weight of 130 pounds, packing the rolls round with the midribs of the sago palm leaf. A heavy load to carry back through swamp, forest, and jungle. Some of this good food, in a glutinous jelly, will be roasted on a slow fire in rolls within its own leaves, mixed with crabs' claws, fish, scraped coconut, and banana. An appetizing meal for any hungry warrior and his family.

So we learn that even a gloomy swamp can be of great use to man. For we have all eaten sago, and know that it is good, and the great swamp lands of New Guinea carry many and many a sago swamp. And wild sugarcane, too, grows in these swamps. How many millions has the sugar industry meant to civilization! Years ago, some of the best of our own Australian sugarcanes came from New Guinea swamps. And we are still searching those swamp lands for new species of sugarcane, and for species that will resist diseases in other lands. As I write this, an American expedition is searching the Sepik for new types of disease-resistant cane; and in years gone by, in the days before malaria began to turn my hair grey, I can remember an American expedition seeking cane away up the Fly.

Many native tribes are agriculturists of no mean order. Centuries ago they took the wild cane and planted and cultivated it in their gardens, together with their bananas, and tobacco, yams, sweet potatoes, coconut palms, kapok-trees, manioc and numerous other vegetables and fruits. Perhaps you have never imagined large villages, with prolific gardens of fruits and vegetables, growing in swamps?

There is another very rich foodstuff growing wild in these vast swamp lands, a food that has kept life in thousands of millions of people for untold centuries. Rice-though, to my limited knowledge, the woolly headed folk do not seem to have cultivated this rice as they have other native foods. Be that as it may, come a moment to the Aramia rice swamps with me: a shallow inland sea of water and land, and a sea of water grasses stretching far away. Dividing the waters are low ridges, all red under sunlight, where new-dug earth peeps out from intense green of cultivation and palms of foliage. The tribesmen, great water men of course, build their villages upon these precious ridges of dry land. And if you could see their lovely gardens, so industriously cultivated, so rich in produce, you would wonder that such men and women could ever be classed as savages.

We are in a canoe poling down a narrow laneway cut through giant grasses, whose sea of heads reaches up feet above the canoe. We know, but cannot see, that away ahead of us is a lovely blue lake, and that over those pretty ridges to our left lies another blue lake; in the bright sky, though, we can see many birds, large birds; but these are nothing to what we can hear all round us as we follow the swamps ever meandering down to the distant river. Hosts of wild geese and ducks, egrets and cranes, birds in baffling variety growing fat and breeding in these rich swamp lands. The long canoe, like a lithe black water-snake, is shooting through a "forest" of rice, of rice plants in ear; with movement of water and canoe, the heads burst and spray the canoe with rice. No wonder the countless waterfowl are so fat. We travel for miles and miles through this forest of wild rice, and if we were away over those ridges we should be travelling through another forest of rice. It is a sea of rice, until the swamps and lakes drain into the Aramia which drains into the Bamu which empties into the Gulf of Papua near the mouth of the Fly.

These rice swamps are far distant from the great swamps of the Fly. Surely we could make some use of them? The grain is not so large as that of cultivated rice, but cultivated rice was Originally grown from wild rice, of course, just as civilized sugarcane has been cultivated from wild swamp sugarcane. Amongst these rice swamps also grows wild flax; and flax also is of considerable use to man.

Over large areas of these swamp lands men, women and children spend half their waking lives upon the water, and many sleep only a few feet above it. Where dry land is scarce and population plentiful, well built bridges span creeks leading from village to village. In such areas, land even a few feet above high water mark is very valuable, both for gardens and village houses. Some villages are built upon stilts, others upon huge beams; others again, as in places along the Fly, are built up in the very trees, only approachable by ladder. Some well-developed tribes build mighty communal houses several hundred feet long, which house groups of families or totem clans, or even the whole village tribe; others build the great Darimu or Long Houses to house the men folk. Such houses are built upon pillars that are the trunks of trees, the Boor 'being often twenty feet above the ground, reached by great notched poles leading up to the platform. The people walk up these poles, sure-footed as monkeys. The taller species of the tough mangrove-trees are often used as building poles and rafters; the Boor is made of split palm laths; the mighty roofs are thatched with sago or nipa palm leaves; the sides generally are strongly made mats of palm leaves. In the earthern fire places the fire is never allowed to go out.

Some villages use a clever device, the reed blowpipe, used for heating coals to fierce blazing point when concentrated heat is needed: the swamp savage centuries ago learnt the secret of the civilized man's forge. Another "invention" is a drill used by the women for boring thread holes through the extremely hard, brilliantly coloured berries and nuts, the shells, wild pig and wallaby teeth, in the making of their necklaces and ornaments. The drill I saw being used years ago was of needle-shaped, hardened bone, or the ivory-plated tooth of a small animal, still further hardened in some way. The drill was fitted, in one case, to a small, strong bow, wound up ingeniously with hair string which, when pulled continuously, "wound up" and released the bow, which revolved the drill with surprising strength and speed. With the addition of a drop of fish oil it was amazing how quickly such a drill would bore through hard materials such as shell and bone. Another drill was worked by both hands and feet, the principle that whirled the drill being the same as that used by a boy when spinning his top-except that as the string ran out it was continuously being re-wound.

Far away up the Fly there was, in my day, an occasional tribe that used a protective armour made of toughened, hardened rattan cane: a well-made cuirass that fitted snugly over chest, stomach and back, as a protection against arrows, densely plaited to offer the greatest resistance to arrow fire. Such work would be fairly easy to people who make those great oval fish traps, so cunningly shaped of plaited cane; the large and small mesh nets, the cleverly woven turtle traps and nets, the wildfowl traps and nets, and the traps and nets for jungle birds spread high up in the branches. You wonder how long ago some dogged fellow first squatted down and laboriously made the tribe's first cuirass. How it must have been examined and criticized as he put it on and stood before those doubting eyes! I wonder did he shout at last, "Fetch your strongest bowman! I will stand as the target! then we shall see!"

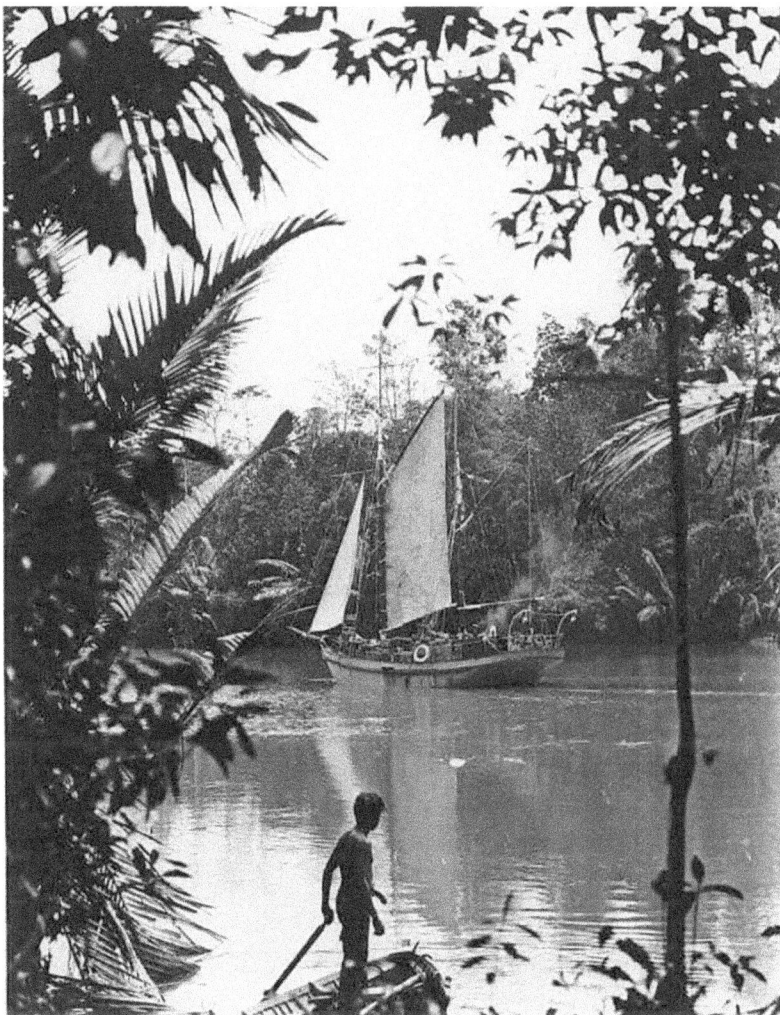

Sailing up the Fly River, by Frank Hurley 1920.

24

COME VISIT THE SEPIK

COME with me to the swamp lands of the Sepik. Surely you have never imagined such a sea of swamps as this, swamps so teeming with life that they support scores of thousands of virile people. Headhunters all, before the Australian Occupation during the 1914-18 war. Learn just a little of what a great swamp can be, and catch a glimpse of the truly miraculous work Australia has accomplished-and that, until the last war, with a mere handful of men.

The Fly and its tributaries rise along the. western watershed of a magnificent mountain range, to flow westward down through Papua. The Sepik rises opposite on the eastern watershed and meanders down through the Mandated Territory. The river mouth is some two miles wide, and in flood the volume of precious water rushing to waste is so powerful that its debris is washed out to sea a hundred miles and more; in flood, too, (and it floods more often than ordinary rivers) its waters spread out over the low-lying country for fifty miles. It has some large tributaries, and countless streams pour from the great mountains down towards and into it. This constant sea of fresh water has for centuries turned many thousands of square miles of low-lying country into swamp lands: the Sepik literally nurses and feeds a sea of swamps, and all the prolific life of plant and fish, bird and man therein.

For many years the Sepik had been known as the mystery river of New Guinea. Then, in 1912, Dr Behrmann headed an expedition and spent two years surveying the main river and tributaries. His map sheets 1, 2, and 3 are a monument to the work achieved. After which the Sepik again lapsed back into mystery, until it was eventually awakened by the superb but unknown work of the Australian administration. The story of the tiny handful of Australians who so swiftly conquered and tamed, so wisely ruled and developed that vast river-swamp territory with its overpowering numbers of virile headhunters would long since have been publicized and acclaimed by all the world if the achievement had been that of any other country.

However, we are speaking of swamps, and the fact that they can be so very different to what we have believed a mere swamp to be. So come with me on a trip up the Sepik, turning back the hand of time and seeing the Sepik of a few years before the last war. We shall beg a lift up river with a Patrol Officer about to set out on a duty patrol-and remember that the things we shall see really happened. We find ourselves chugging up river in a tiny Government pinnace manned by half a dozen alert and efficient Police Boys, steaming up along the bank, for the midstream current would sweep us back again. The wide stretch of brownish water rolls sullenly past between walls of gigantic "pit-pit" (cane grass), and for a week or more we shall be passing through great forests of gigantic grasses, with the fronds of sacsac palms and patches of dense scrub behind them. As we near Singarin village a floating grass island comes bearing down upon us, a fine big kapiak-tree growing in its very centre. Birds call cheekily from the floating islet as, warily, we chug past. Fortunately the head boat boy is keeping a sharp look-out for a much greater danger, one that comes invisibly, camouflaged under masses of russet brown debris and entangled water plants. Had that enormous log rammed the pinnace it would have smashed it like an eggshell!

In late afternoon we pass Marienberg, a picturesque Government sub-station and a relief to the eye, set high upon a big coral limestone ridge: just a cluster of native-built houses, coconut palms gracefully outlined above the bulk store, the rest houses and petrol dump. The P.O's quarters, the police and native barracks, look neat and shipshape. This little station represents invincible power to the thousands of turbulent natives scattered all over the Lower Sepik. Thus Patrol Officer Eric Robinson (at this particular time) with fifteen Police Boys is rapidly taming a huge and difficult area, as other isolated men, widely scattered through the great Territory, are laboriously but surely exploring it, then bringing it under control, gradually reaching out over area after area; as other men, years and years before, started out to tame adjoining Papua.

We pass the mission station controlled by Father Kirchbaum, who is so bound up in the pioneer story of the Lower Sepik. Groves of coconut palms wave here above a sea of kuni grass. The P.O. has a job ashore here. You follow him for several miles along a track through dense kuni covering undulating country. In that primeval land the throbbing echo of an oil boring plant comes as a surprise-and here are Captain Hanlin and driller Crawford and crew, boring for oil. They invite you to kai-kai; and after lunch young Hyde of Amalgamated Wireless comes whistling along and declares the opportunity too good to miss: so you sit down to a prosaic game of bridge. But soon you are chugging upstream again to dine before sundown, then ready to dive in under the mosquito net. For the Sepik after sundown is a world of mosquitoes; it is difficult to believe that even the armour-plated crocodiles can survive out of water. Poke your head out of the mosquito net and you suddenly realize man is not the Invincible Master he fondly believes himself to be.

In many a village, too, there is a rush now for the sleeping baskets-great long baskets of finely plaited cane into which the whole family crawl. The mother with her babe first; then father, who butts her gently with his head if the mosquitoes are coming in too; then the eldest son, unless he has attained the age and dignity of a basket all to himself; then the eldest girl. The youngest girl crawls in last and woe betide her if she does not turn the end of the basket under securely against the ravening mosquitoes.

Some villages possess enormous baskets, actually community sleeping baskets, which hold thirty or forty people, and a pig or two. One of the difficult and pointless rules of the unpredictable white man, once he has gained control of a village, is that pet pigs are forbidden to sleep with the family. Whoever heard of such a thing? The favourite pig that the warrior's wife herself suckled in its baby days!

And so we chug along through the Lower Sepik, the riverbanks beautiful at times, with patches of jungle or scrub gay with drooping curtains of scarlet flowers that festoon in graceful ropes from tree to tree. Among the masses of kunda vines and convolvulus a pretty Cari pigeon, big as a plump fowl, is pridefully showing off his topknot. Other pigeon beauties are crooning among the berries; parrots flash by in vivid clouds of colour. Now the river-banks appear as a sea of pit-pit grass above which seem to float the palm fronds of sac-sac swamps. The pinnace heads in through a narrow channel hedged in by rustling pit-pit grass until we creep out into a lagoon startlingly beautiful with its sheet of scarlet and white water lilies so densely covering the water that the tall brown houses of Imbandu village can throw no reflection even at the very edge of the water. The air is heavy-scented from flowers, noisy. from wildfowl. The natives cheerfully come to meet the Patrol Officer headed by the Luluai (Chief), who is closely followed by the tul-tul (henchman and interpreter). A jolly crowd, these folk, with their laughing-eyed curiosity, fine features, good physique, coppery coloured skin, each coquettish girl wearing an excellently woven and dyed pul-pul (grass skirt) fitted so well to show off her plump, well-made thighs. Easy to see at a glance here the white man's guiding hand in the health of the people, the cleanly kept village, and the absence of that fear, so recently ever present of headhunters. Coconut and the graceful betel-nut palm wave above the kapiak trees and vivid yellow-green of well-kept banana gardens that merge back into dense sac-sac, the sago palms. The well-built houses are set high on piles, for during high water a lake Bows under the house Boors. The canoes are strikingly picturesque with carvings of crocodiles, pigs, dogs, and birds. The surprising speed with which the Lower Sepik has already been tamed is curiously shown among practically all the lower river villages by the absence of carvings of note. They have already been "traded" to recruiters and missionaries and shipped to the museums of the world.

When passing Angorum village the P.O. nods and says, "Once the site of a German Government station." The brown-skinned men stand silently watching as the pinnace steams past; you wonder what their thoughts are.

Would they rather have the Germans as masters, or the Australians? Or would they rather be their own, in constant danger of losing their heads to stronger neighbours?

Thus on past the mouth of the Keram tributary and on to Magendo village with its brown women and prolific gardens. And night.

Farther up river and the pinnace noses away from the main stream into a "round water", a lagoon, chugging along through a chain of lagoons, so rank with grasses that we see a natural example of how this titanic sea of grass is, or appears to be, slowly but surely choking the big river. Crocodiles seem to be lying about almost anywhere, birds in screeching thousands rise from the water-lilies. Not the only wild things, for we catch a glimpse of loaded canoes racing away through passages in the grass. Thus they fled Kumbarumba village. The houses built over black and stagnant water in which pigs grunt as they wallow. And here we must wait awhile for the Patrol Officer sends out his scout boys to get in touch with the frightened people. With tact and patience, if not this trip then the next he must win these timid people's confidence until finally he convinces them the white man means them no harm, but much good.

An impressive sight of savage building power is their "House Tamboran", towering on huge piles, its length two hundred feet. This is their "sacred house", their spirit house where the secret initiation ceremonies take place. We climb the rickety steps leading up to the floor of Limbon and black palm, treading gingerly lest we crash down into the black water fifteen feet below. Around the gloomy walls hang gigantic masks with fearful human faces most realistically carved. Bamboo flutes and carved instruments of bone and wood are half glimpsed within the corners of mat-work cubicles. Fires are still smouldering on beds of clay. Odd bones lie about, unguessable things are half seen in gloomy corners. Grisly weapons lie everywhere. It is joy to get out into the lovely sunlight again.

A great contrast such a beastly, filthy, mosquito-plagued village to those many others that the white man has already got under control, so very different, for instance, to the healthy, grass-cleaned, well-fenced, pig-proof, and almost mosquito-less village of Magendo. But this village also will be cleaned up in time.

Past the mouth of the Just tributary we come to the villages of Kambrindo and Krinjambi. We camp for the night at Kanduanum, startled to hear the weird, high-pitched wailing call for the dead. For a crocodile that morning had taken the tul-tul's baby son. We camp in" the neatly constructed "House Kiap" which every village when brought under control must build and keep in order for the use of government officials and travellers. In dismal hopelessness that death wail haunts our sleep.

25

THE HEADHUNTERS' LAND

.ABOARD again next morning and away, sunlight on the sullen brown river is cheerful indeed as the death wail slowly fades astern. The Patrol Officer whips up his rifle and "Bang!" - a crocodile on a sandbank lashes out with its tail and rolls over with paws clutching skyward as vainly it tries to roll back into the. water. A yell of frantic delight from the crew boys, for we had so soon avenged the spirit of the tul-tul's son. But presently superstition again clouds their eyes as over those miles and miles of grasses, rolling down over the surge of waters, comes the sinister boom of a giant garramut. These huge slit gongs, fashioned from the hollowed trunks of trees, spread news with astounding rapidity over thousands of square miles of river and swamp.

We have left the tamed sophistication of the Lower Sepik natives astern and are now within the land of the headhunters, the fast-growing boom of their garramuts spreading news of our coming far and wide. You sense an uneasily tense atmosphere amongst the crew boys as presently the tall coconut palms of Tambanum and Womban tower above the grass sea ahead. These are the first villages of the Middle River "talk".

Tambanum is, at the time of our trip, a much dreaded and the most powerful village known on the Sepik. It commands considerable areas of fertile country with extensive gardens, a picture of experienced agriculture. Its men, especially well developed from the hips up because of the constant paddle work, are strong, intelligent-looking brutes, deigning a half-hidden scowl, or just an indifferent glance at the approaching white men. You feel pleased now that the wary, efficient-looking Police Boys are well-armed. Surrounding the big village is a strong fence, almost invisible against the tall pit-pit grass outside it. Inside are many large, well-built houses, high up on solid piles. Everywhere through this great area you see practical evidence of man against the ever-present danger-water! Myriad palms lift feathery heads up to a bright sky; you gaze puzzled, for they appear like titanic pot-plants, their roots standing firmly planted upon large mounds built up five feet high above the earth.

This is to protect them when first planted from flood waters. Very many papaw, loaded with rich, yellowish-red fruit, stand prettily with numerous loulou-trees amongst the towering palms.

With his bodyguard the Luluai strolls forward to greet the Patrol Officer. He is as venerable and dignified an old devil as ever hacked off his fellow-man's head. The story of this smiling old wretch's life would be a story of life-long cunning, of swift canoe raids by night, of burning villages and massacre, and other nasty things. His hair falls in long ringlets pridefully oiled. A beautiful black "bokis" drapes his savage loins. This skirt of flying-fox skins is the insignia of a highly successful headhunter. For he who has taken a head wears the flying-fox skin. So proud are they of this that even the white man can sense on occasion how they draw back with a stare of arrogant supremacy at their too closely pressing naked comrades.

Wearing picturesque headdresses ornamented with shells in bright patterns, glorious with brilliant bird of paradise plumes and snow-white osprey plumes, these brown headhunters walk with the swing and confident bearing of conquerors. Why shouldn't they! For they have conquered their world, they have decimated or brought into terrified submission whole tribes of inland swamp men for a great area around them. You experience an uneasy feeling that too plainly many are showing their intention not to cringe to us.

You accompany the P.O. in state to the House Kiap, with the Luluai and tul-tul. For the P.O. is here to see that orders from the last visit have been carried out-you don't envy him.

In the House Kiap is kept the Village Book, at the period of your visit regarded with a superstitious sullenness, for it is believed that this strange thing can "talk-talk", can tell the Patrol Officer those things done which were ordered not to be done, and those things not done which were ordered to be done.

All along the big river and throughout its great area of swamp lands wherever a village has been brought under control it has been issued a Village Book by the District Officer. When a census has been taken the names of all inhabitants are herein written in their respective family groups. This Village Book, sacredly kept in the House Kiap, is henceforth in rigid charge of the Luluai. In addition to the families, census, and other matters, the Kiap (otherwise the District Officer) records his instructions to the Luluai in the back of the book, orders to be carried out regarding sanitation, making of roadways, planting of crops and coconuts, fencing in of the village, the cutting of grass for health and cleanliness and eradication of mosquitoes, the keeping of pigs *outside* the village fence, prompt burial of the dead, cessation of headhunting, feuds, adjudication of quarrels, and medical and other administrative details - such as instructions that, to provide for the future, all parents of newly born children must plant ten coconut palms for each child; and that, to encourage families, fathers of four living children by one wife should be exempt from payment of the capitation tax (assessed in this village and at this time at 10s a year).

In succeeding visits by the Kiap (D.O.) and Patrol Officer these instructions are checked up and any failure to comply is understandingly and promptly dealt with.

Standing listening there to the reverberating boom of the garramut vibrating through the matting walls, with the animal-like smell of wild men in your nostrils, you begin to realize what a striking page of civilization has been thus so simply introduced into the mind and heart of savage man by this Village Book. Pages not written in crimson by lead bullets and steel - but how quick, simple, and effective. Pages, too, all for the villagers' good. These people will not die in forced labour, never in slave gangs.

The business of the P.O. having been carried out in due earnestness and solemnity, you are at liberty for a glance at the village. But-do not meddle. First, a gigantic new House Tamboran in the course of construction has caught your eye, its towering bulk overshadows all. It would have been joyfully completed quite a time ago but for the determined interference of the accursed white man, the power that has so unaccountably interfered with the age-old, normal life of the river. For this same power has firmly decreed that on no account must any heads be taken to consecrate the new House Tamboran. And when a House Tamboran cannot be blooded, why then it is no House Tamboran at all! In bewildered sullenness they feel that the strange white man, though there is only one of him here and there up and down river, somehow possesses the real power to carry out this order-to prevent a bloody christening.

Wondering at its gigantic proportions, you stare up at the roof timbers and poles already in position. The main posts are full-grown trees two feet in diameter, the branches lopped off at the first large fork. Carvings of crocodiles ten feet long crawl around them, standing out in relief, as if raging to climb. Very terrible things had been planned to happen to those selected river people who should fail to defend themselves effectually when this gigantic House Tamboran had been completed. You would risk the climb up for a peep inside, but you sense the atmosphere is perhaps not quite favourable.

A broad-shouldered, sullen-looking savage is beating a garramut. Propped up on chocks, it is the hollowed, sawn-off trunk of a tree. A genius has been displayed in its fashioning, both as to proportion and shape to produce a sound that will carry long distances, and in the imagery and finish of its carvings, the hideously gaping jaws of crocodiles, fierce snouts of wild boars, perfect flight of birds. There seems a twisted genius, too, in the grotesque but frighteningly lifelike forms of the man with the pig's head, the writhing crocodile snout upon a man's body, the combination of humans and animals and birds, each carving possessing symbolical meaning to tribal Tambus, each weird picture telling a hereditary story to the initiated.

The dread boom of these garramuts had for unknown years terrorized the villages far and wide, foretelling the toll of death to many a shivering wretch throughout the distant swamps. This powerful village had resisted Government control for years and at the time of our visit had only recently been brought definitely under control. And the Administration officers have experienced a hectic time keeping a sharp eye on these warlike people, still sullenly determined on blooding the terrible house. It has meant ceaseless vigilance on the part of the Administration, a great patience and understanding and mental and physical courage on the part of the handful of District and Patrol Officers to prevent them from doing so.

Hounded on by the older warriors saturated by centuries of blood-letting and mysticism, the young warriors were raging to distinguish themselves in a slaughter throughout all swamps within reach, to return triumphantly in their bloodstained canoes with the grisly heads to christen the great spirit house, to the thunder of the garramuts, the hysterical excitement of the girls. Thus each young warrior had been longing and longing for his chance to win and wear the coveted flying-fox skin. Had you come within reach of this village but a very few years previously your own head quite possibly would have found itself grinning down from high up in a niche in the gigantic roof.

You realize now that life in the swamps, in some swamps at least, can be very different to what you have believed life in a swamp to be.

However, you have been learning things. Right away west in Papua, before a tiny handful of men similarly tamed the wild folk there, the gigantic Dubu houses used to be very similarly christened - among some tribes, with variations. Trees would be cut down, and the trunks chopped off for the supports for the great house to be. Round, deep holes would be dug to take these huge piles. Then the village warriors would depart 'on a man hunt. Wretched prisoners would be dragged back, unharmed.

Down into each hole that was to be the bed of a main pile a wretched prisoner was carefully pushed, feet first, alive.

Then the huge pile was lowered down on top of him.

But here you are in Tambanum village on the Middle Sepik, the thunderous voice of the garramut booming out news of the P.O's arrival and you wonder what else beside. Upon a scowling group of warriors near by you admire exquisitely carved kumbungs, the bamboo containers or calabash gourds used for carrying lime for betel-nut chewing. To these are attached lime sticks from which hang minute chains of plaited grass tasselled with brilliant feathers. Each tassel represents the head of a man taken in fight. Their spears are monstrous hafts twelve feet long cut from Limbon and Quela wood. These could kill a bullock, let alone a man. Most warriors are smeared with guak oil. This prized oil is extracted from some unknown tree. A hole is cut in the heart. Within three months the little well fills with oil. It is highly valued for curative properties. During initiation, when tribal designs are cut into the skins of young men, the wounds are rubbed with the oil. On healing, the skin is raised in rope-like weals.

You have time for a quick "look-see" down the village, surprised to see that it appears to be a mile in length. The well-built, roomy houses are ornamented with numerous carvings. Women of all ages are busy everywhere, mostly in gossiping groups, their eyes quick for the visitors; as you stroll along you hear some girlish remark greeted with laughter that you feel uncomplimentary to yourself. The women are beautifully proportioned, with eyes large and brown and impudent. The belles of the village are a mixture of the coquette, the cat, and the devil-you've an uneasy feeling the latter predominates. Each unmarried girl wants a man, and the man she is determined to marry is a man who has taken a head. Then she will feel certain she will bear sons who will be killers of men. Each wears a pul-pul, a short grass skirt expertly woven. It is fluffy, soft to the skin, patterned and dyed and fitted with telling effect. They wear bright necklaces, their firm, rounded arms adorned with armbands of clinking shells; ornaments of brilliant feathers and berries draw further attention to their shapely legs. They are attractive little she-devils, these whose life's ambition is to wed a man-killer and bear sons who will take the heads of men.

Many are busy at weaving the great cane sleeping baskets which are eagerly traded for by the river villagers. They eye you roguishly as their nimble fingers work so skilfully to make these baskets mosquito proof. Others are frying the family's sago roll or cake in neat little clay frying pans. Yet others are mixing paint materials in beautifully carved utensils, some are coconut shell which has been sawn in half. Yet others are shaving the youngsters' heads with a sliver of bamboo, which, when split expertly, leaves a razor keen edge. The youngsters are smoking with all the assurance of the men and women, rolling their cigarettes of native tobacco in banana-leaf wrappings. Eagerly they crowd round you, though, for any old newspaper or magazine, that luxurious cigarette paper. Swiftly they have learnt the difference between banana leaf and newspaper as cigarette paper. Surprising what a great influence little things like this exert in hastening the civilizing of a savage people!

You have noticed this large village is scrupulously clean, the people particularly healthy. And the dreaded Frambosia even now has been almost wiped out by injections of N.A.B.

As regretfully you return to the launch you begin to realize the great work done in such a short time by the very few District and Patrol Officers, to bring under control, and into health, so many villages such as this. As again the launch is chugging up river the P.O. explains that medical relief has proved one of the Administration's strongest weapons in helping to bring the Sepik's warlike thousands under control, for quickly the "magic" of modern medical treatment gained the confidence of the natives in the good intentions of the white man. After the first difficult preliminary work in taming a new village an intelligent "boy" is chosen, taken away to District Headquarters, and given six months' careful training at the Native Hospital. He then receives a hat as badge of office and proudly arrives back in his village as the "Medical Tul-tul". He is supplied with castor oil, Condy's, boracic acid, quinine, bandages, and other simple medicines and medical aids. The medical tul-tuls often become quite proficient. As the village is brought fully under control the tul-tul gains full authority, in case of urgent sickness or severe wounds, to commandeer help and hurry the patient away to the nearest Native Hospital. He can also order any native to hospital for needed medical attention. The striking results attained, the relief from so many common chronic illnesses, soon make a deep impression on the native mind.

You are being borne along upon a sullen brown river. Far ahead, almost right to the great mountains, and far to either side, is a sea of gigantic grasses and water. Far away out there are thousands of headhunters who never yet have seen a white man. You begin to realize that the difficulties of Administration can only be guessed at by the outsider. Firstly, a new district is more or less roughly mapped out on paper. Then it has to be penetrated, explored. Then, village by village the people must be taught to cease headhunting, then cease just ordinary murder. Then they are trained to plant their "natural" dead in a cemetery, rather than under the house. Then they must clear their village of grass to help keep down the mosquitoes, then fence the village to keep out the pigs that live with them. They are taught they must not spear Patrol Officers, or any white man, or· any man at all. They must be taught that the white man's medicine is much more powerful than their witchcraft and sorcery. They must be taught many, many other things before that village can be mapped as "under control".

It is all very bewildering to the poor puzzled headhunter, this sudden, complete change in the way of life that has been his and his fathers' for thousands of years. It must seem to him as it might seem to us if a few strange men from Mars dropped down amongst us and, by using some fantastic, unknown power compelled our millions utterly to change our beliefs and way of life.

Yes, bewildering to the headhunter, and often heartbreaking to the white man. But it is a man's work and the last few years since this trip have been rewarded by truly marvellous results.

When you set out to think about swamps you thought-why, you thought a swamp was just a swamp!

Kanduanum is the last village in the Marienberg Division, Tambanum the first in the Ambunti, into which district the launch pushes upstream against the brown river boiling viciously but so silently past. The silence of those rolling waters could get on a fever-sick man's nerves, the everlasting pit-pit grass dense on the banks, wild sugarcane and jungle alternately, and upon the waters great patches of the kango, an edible creeper. White herons fish quietly along the grass-grown bends, a kingfisher darts past like a living emerald, wild ducks in Hocks, sulphur-crested cockatoos screech at the launch from the jungle patches, the big black cockatoo in heavy Hight Haps raucously overhead. Plovers run with fairy steps over the mudbanks, the lotus bird runs daintily across the broad lily leaves.

Your boys are mostly Buka and Manus men who can converse in shouted "pidgin" as you pass by a little village. Hence ever and anon there comes shooting out from the grass-lined bank a canoe filled with eager savages bringing bananas, yams, a pig, papaws, and sugarcane for trade but particularly for money!

The cessation of headhunting by thousands of men in the big area then brought under control created a great vacancy in these men's lives. Trading fortunately stepped in to help fill the vacancy, trade now rapidly taking the place of hunting for heads. And so swiftly does "civilization" follow upon the first firm steps of control you are surprised at these eager, grinning savages hungry for money. It helps to pay their head tax!

The headhunter's energies are now diverted - to work, and to trading the products of his work. Fortunately, he suddenly finds he likes trading.

And quietly, for just once in your life you bless a tax - the headhunters' head tax. For not quite four years back these very same men with blood-curdling yells would have sped out to you, not for barter, but for your heads!

26

THE RIVER AND THE GRASSES

So interesting days roll by despite monotony of water amongst far-flung forests. of grass, broken only by occasional muffled, muttered drumming or the glimpse of a beautiful bird, despite the ever-present breath of the swamps, the hum of the mosquito terror nights. By day the brown water, logs and debris rolling past the pinnace, a crocodile sliding down from the bank, palm tops of a new village appearing round the bend. Maybe thunder clouds gathering, otherwise an ocean of clear blue so very high up. The main river now has narrowed to a width of three quarters of a mile, but is a mighty stream yet. Occasionally, from somewhere far within the great swamps extending away to every side, comes the harsh, sinister boom of a garramut, muffled by distance-calling the people to feast after the taking of heads, most likely, far back in that mysterious distance where thousands of the swamp men do not yet even know the name of the white man.

The boom of a friendly or indifferent garramut heralds your approach to a village. And before departure the news will be boomed upstream. Thus the pinnace can never come upon any river village by surprise.

And you had never known there was such a river of swamps in the whole wide world, let alone that this world of swamps was controlled by Australia.

Easy to pick out those village "boys" who have been away down to coast and island areas on "indentured labour"; their skin has a healthy sheen from cleanlier habits, plenty of food and soap. Such boys are travellers and give themselves superior airs. But then, I've known white travellers do the same. Maybe you will, I hope unconsciously, when you go home and tell them "all about the Sepik".

The pinnace heads towards a large creek pouring into the Sepik in wild current rips and lash of swirling waters with a rising hum. On both banks of the creek is built the large village of Tumbungu. The men are arrogant, powerful brutes, but intelligent with it. Like the men of Tambanum they have in the past vigorously resented the advent of

"Government". But now they have among them a mighty traveller and real medicine man, their own medical tul-tul. He is a cheerful cuss who poles his canoe all over the place while standing on one leg like a solemn crane. The other leg was amputated in Rabaul. And the breathless tales he told his people on return about that great wonder "White Man Village" Rabaul, and the number and supernatural powers of the white men there had quite a bearing in curbing his sullen tribesmen.

Farther upstream and the pinnace pulls in to a bend in the river, greeted by many eager people at the pretty village of Angerman, surrounded by thick scrub, a newly constructed fence enclosing. it. These merry inhabitants are eager to trade; you feel sorry you are only in a tiny pinnace and so far from civilization, for the plentiful array of weapons, ornaments, and utensils are beautifully carved. Even the skins of the men and women are marked in exceptionally fine designs. The House Tamboran as usual attracts you, but here there seems something unusual. Out from the gigantic house is a long clearing which has been banked up with earth to some three feet in height. In the centre stands a circular mound about seven feet across, bound together by riveted logs. Coconut palms, hibiscus, and prettily decorative trees flourish upon this mound. Sentinelled round these stand large splinters of moss-stained stone, symbols of some long forgotten cult of ages past.

The Angerman tribesmen, through the interpreter, solemnly give a name to each stone. But they know nothing more. They have no knowledge whatever of what these stones represented to the vanished people who erected them in the long dim past, no legend even of who those people were.

As the pinnace chugs up stream you wonder a moment. Already the river has absorbed you, you feel its cool, grassy breath, its mighty swamps and booming garramuts and the cruel House Tamboran and bird life and the crocodile and the fierce natives have been here for ever. But here is mute evidence that some other race lived and exulted in their traditions and deep, mysterious beliefs upon this sea of swamps long before the present race of natives came.

Whence came the first comers? And were they the first?

Whence came the present race?

You remember then, in distant but adjoining Papua, on the old alluvial goldfields, the queer stone pestles and mortars and other curios found down under many feet of earth when the goldminers were sinking shafts. The present day Papuans know nothing of the vanished people who made and used those stone utensils.

Who were *they*?

Upon the ever rolling river under that mighty sky such thoughts make you feel very small. You shrug them away with a mental, "Who knows?" And inevitably the question follows, "What am I, anyway?"

Still farther upstream the pinnace bow turns towards the bank to nose carefully into a narrow, grass-lined channel where lovely trees arch overhead. But presently the everlasting grass slows down, stops the launch as it slowly but surely is beating the mighty river itself. But is it? For this river must have Bowed for untold ages. For vast lengths of time it has been one mighty struggle between the river and the forests of giant grasses. Surely it is that the river must hold the final balance of power, otherwise it would have been choked long, long ago.

To the long-drawn yells of your crew boys come answering yells, musical through the grass. Soon afterward a canoe manned by paddling natives comes swiftly along the grass-grown channel. You step cautiously aboard and with triumphal song are canoed for half a mile through the grass to their village of Mindimbit.

Years ago this village, like many others, was situated on the river bank. But with the imperceptible change of the river course grass is now growing where the river once flowed. The main stream is now nearly a mile away.

The Patrol Officer's business finished, you carry on up river, becoming increasingly aware of the merciless, ceaseless struggle between the giant grasses and the river. The spreading roots, the enormous tonnage of seed from the giant grass-heads yearly falling into the water to sink to the bottom mud, germinate, take root, then struggle up, up, up to at last thrust a vigorous head above water, over thousands of square miles, for untold seasons, extending, thickening, ever encroaching upon the river's water space.

Where it has triumphed, as by the village of Mindimbit and over many and many another area, the river has still beaten it by changing direction, many times, perhaps only slightly. The water in mighty pressure has heaved down along the weaker bank and bowed down the grass. If only its volume and pressure can hold down the grass-heads there long enough then those heads, choking for sunlight and air, must smother and drown.

What a titanic struggle it has been, ever is, must be, how frightening the ceaselessness of it!

If it had not been for the constant volume of water pouring down from the mighty mountain system into the Sepik Valley, the great river itself would have been smothered long ago, of course. But that enormous volume of water keeps surging down and irresistibly demands a travelling route for over five hundred miles to the sea. The mountains feeding the river, the low country feeding the grasses.

Never-ending war between river and grasses - ceaseless war between mountains and plain!

As the launch pushes on up against the current you feel a new respect for this living brown water surging so fiercely past. It possesses a relentless purpose, and a life other than you dreamed of.

Suddenly a surprised cry, "Sail oh!" The pinnace crew excitedly shout, "Kiap he come!" and you gaze at a neat, fast-travelling pinnace coming out of the Sud River just ahead.

Jauntily she flies the Australian blue ensign. Sighting you, she wheels and comes speeding downstream. Thus you meet the Government pinnace *Osprey* in a neat coat of white and grey, a pretty craft, complete with mosquito proof cabin, and obviously efficient. Standing smartly at attention on the forepeak is a sergeant of Native Police and two constables in uniform, white-covered cap, blue "lap-lap" gay with narrow red band above pointed edges round the hem, a bright red cummerbund round the waist. Each is armed with service rifle and bayonet. A military looking bos'n stands ready beside a rope; he is dressed in a khaki lap-lap on which is a broad red band and the design of an anchor in a circle.

You stare, and wonder if you are dreaming. Have you been miraculously transferred to some grim African river where the noble white man sternly carries his burden?

No, you are on the Sepik, where a handful of your own Australians have quietly been doing the job for some time past, where in adjoining Papua they similarly have been doing it away back when you were a schoolboy - and before that!

The pinnace is caught in the wash of the *Osprey* as she comes neatly up alongside. You see in the fore cabin a half-caste Malay at the wheel.

"Prisoners!" murmurs the P.O., as you see aboard seven or eight wild-looking men from the swamps. Naked, excepting two who wear the significant flying-fox skins. Their long hair, twisted into pencil-thick coils smothered in coconut oil, is held in place by bands worked in intricate designs of. cowrie shells. Several wear a short bamboo stick through the septum of the nose, others slivers of pearlshell. All wear necklaces of shells. From the lime stick of a Luluai hang five finely plaited grass chains with tassels of red, white, and blue feathers - proof positive that he has taken five heads. They stare sombrely; you feel they would love to cut your throat.

By a cabin at the stern where hang bunches of bananas, papaws, and pineapples ripening in the sunlight, sits an officer spick and span in white, complete with collar, tie, and helmet upon which shines the brass badge of "Government". Again you remember boyhood stories of "Deeds of Empire", surprised that this really is an Australian picture in a setting of New Guinea savagery. But the first words of the white officer are typically Australian.

"Got any mail?" The spell is broken.

Both officers exchange greetings and you meet the District Officer, Colonel H. E. Woodman, D.S.D., Headquarters at Ambunti, on the Upper Sepik.

Stones in swamps in the Upper Sepik, 1919.

27

THE EMBARRASSING HEADHUNTER

THE D.O. invites the P.O. and you, too, to join him at kai-kai at Kumindimbit, the next village upstream. Both pinnaces steam ahead, but soon the "boss" representative of Australian law and order leaves you far behind.

"The *Osprey* can travel," remarks the P.O. admiringly, "but then the D.O. is driving her; he is quick-smart when there is a job to be done."

The D.O. had arranged to mark out a new village for natives who had Bed their homes on the Kosameri, owing to headhunting raids. When you met him he was returning from investigating the scene on the bank of the Kosameri River, where some little time previously the Kosameri people had been surprised by the Kumindimbit in a howling massacre-well planned. Away from the main village, the Kosameri had been occupying a sac-sac camp on the river bank. At daylight they were awakened from sleep by stabbing spears and thud of clubs. Twenty-four heads had been taken before the people fled. The usual evidence lay rotting there. Not much. Only a few scattered bones of the headless bodies, for crocodiles and dogs and pigs had made short work of everything eatable. Just a few bones, and pul-puls, leg- and arm-bands trampled in the mud, broken weapons. All the cooking pots smashed, all things smashed in the mad frenzy. Nothing left now but the deep sigh of the grasses, the vicious mosquito chorus by night.

In a search for survivors the D.O. had hurried far up the headwaters of that tributary, well past the last spot surveyed by Dr Behrmann, right on until the waters shallowed into a maze of snags. But no sign of survivors.

Lower down river than the scene of massacre the people of two small villages had abandoned their homes. And it was for these that the D.O. had promised to mark out a new village site, in a position at which the "White Man Law" at Ambunti could pro-tect them, also come swiftly to their aid if necessary. You see the preliminary work now as the pinnace chugs on, for there, away across on the bank, is the white-suited form of the D.O. busy with the compass and marking poles, his Police Boys supervising a crowd of men, women, and children busily clearing the grass. Thus the D.O. will mark out for the Luluai the places of the new homes for the people. In a miraculously short time a new village will spring up, and one too that, by the irony of Fate, the headhunters themselves have automatically "brought under control".

You may be "certain sure" these frightened people will cling to the white man's protection and law.

Just as your pinnace is arriving at Kumindimbit village the *Osprey* overtakes you. The Police Boys leap ashore, swiftly erect a long bamboo mast, and hoist the flag to a smart, "Present Arms!"

As you watch this unfolding scene story after forgotten story of empire-building comes hazily to mind. Strange that you have never known, never heard that Australia with her tiny population, for long years past has been doing the very same work. But without the fanfare of world trumpets, without the selfish, fabulous commercial gain, and without the river of blood that the "bringing under control" of native races in other lands has known. Compared to what has occurred in other lands Australia has hardly spilt one drop of native blood in bringing under control her great heritage of Papua, the Mandated Territory, and numerous adjoining islands. And there has been no exploitation, the work has been for the natives themselves. Perhaps even a little too much so.

A table and folding chair is placed under the flag, the D.O. takes the salute, then quickly gets to work conducting an inquiry regarding the latest massacre. The sullen-looking Luluai and all his leading men are there, the villagers gather silently round. Many in turn are interrogated. The patience, firmness, and tact needed to drag out helpful and truthful detail is soon obvious.

For there come as answers a maze of evasions, deliberate lies, and beating about the bush. Very soon you realize these natives possess brains, and can cunningly use them. All questions and answers must be sifted by means of an interpreter, and put on paper.

But the D.O. has a very strong string to his bow. For the ringleaders in the massacre had already been ferreted out and arrested, and brought to Ambunti by canoe with the twenty-four heads as exhibits. A very fine piece of work, so the D.O. explains to the P.O. later, on the part of Corporal Bellekiei of the Native Police and three constables. An exceptionally fine piece of work, the D.O. adds, work requiring courage, initiative, tact, endurance and unshakeable determination. Few white officers could have done the job so well. As the D.O. talks his eyes shine, you can tell by his voice he is very proud of his Police Boys.

You feel he is justified, as you hear the sigh of the grass over these vast swamp lands that stretch far inland to the mountains, far away back to the sea. How those wild headhunters could have been tracked and actually caught in all this wilderness under the amazing conditions of these rivers and swamps and vengeful hostility astonishes you.

But, step by step, life must be made-safe for the thousands of frightened ones cringing along these rivers and swamps. The representatives of tribes will soon see with their own eyes that the white man's authority is in earnest. And angrily the garramuts, along hundreds of miles of river, and far away out over the great swamps will be booming their loud, harsh news of yet another setback to the headhunters' vanishing rule of terror and blood.

Whilst the Kiap was busy with his police investigation puzzle, his cook boys had been busy on a matter of far more moment than the fate of a few headhunters. You appreciate their point of view as you sit down to an excellent meal of soup, wild pigeon, roast fowl (bought for a shilling per head) yams, native cabbage, fresh bread tasty from yeast made from the milk of green coconut, baked in the camp oven. This is followed up with freshly picked bananas, papaws, watermelon and pineapples.

You wonder at this most appetizing meal, so cheap, too, in the heart of this great swamp land so far from civilization. But you have already seen this land which above water will luxuriantly grow almost anything. You never dreamt that swamp life could be like this, now did you?

The people have vanished, the village strangely, deathly quiet.

They are shocked, shocked that the white man can not only catch their warrior headhunter heroes, but actually arrest them! They seem numbed; they do not know what to do about it.

Thankful are you that they feel just that way. You count up the pitiful number of firearms in this actually reinforced party, and wonder at what can be the strange fear of the white man that holds these hundreds of sullenly thwarted headhunters at bay. If they should make but one determined rush then it would be all over in a few minutes.

With the setting of the sun comes a terror greater than headhunters. You dive for the mosquito net as the night is taken over by the winged battalions. You gratefully know that the headhunters and their families will in snarling hurry also be driven into their sleeping baskets. You sleep peacefully in that village which but a few days before had been a howling bedlam in the triumphal celebrations of headhunters now hushed in uneasy silence, for the Kiap, who is the White Man Law, has come.

Next morning the *Osprey* speeds fast up stream. Your little launch follows, but the P.O. must "run the rule" over Kararau village, which some time ago was the scene of a particularly bloodthirsty headhunting orgy. So the pinnace noses its way into a lagoon which years ago was the actual course of the river, now beaten back past here by the grasses. The P.O. finds all quiet at Kararau village and the pinnace makes its way back to the river and chugs upstream again to Tegoi. Thankfully you all stay the night at the House Kiap. Wild sugarcane here grows in profusion. Morning time, and you are walking along a picturesque track through dense bush ideal for ambuscade.

Somewhat uneasily you carefully follow directly behind the boy close ahead, half expecting any moment to hear the agonized yell of one falling down into a pit. For you know now that such defence pits in areas are dug in approaches to villages. Such a pit may be nine feet deep, toothed with spears whose barbed points stick up at such angles that a man falling in must be impaled. When camouflaged in the kuni flats the dense tussocks completely hide the cruel menace. Around the mouth of a new pit the natives plant grass and vines which immediately grow and quickly trellis into a mass of herbage over the pit. Such pits are also used as traps for wild pig and wallaby. Even along a well-trodden path, thickly walled with jungle, there may be such a defence trap - and particularly cleverly disguised of necessity here. A "lid" is made of plaited cane, reeds, or twigs to cover the pit mouth as a trapdoor. Decomposed leaves are spread over the lid, then loam. And across that loam is cleverly pressed the plain, inviting imprint of the pad. Some New Guinea villages are encircled by such traps, regarded as a first line of defence.

"Cunning devils!" you think, and tread warily indeed at times, feeling the hidden meaning in "like a cat walking on hot bricks"!

You emerge on the bank of a long lagoon and there stands out a large village of well constructed houses overshadowed by a giant House Tamboran. The ceaselessly growing grass seems rapidly advancing over the waters of the lagoon, swallowing it up, smothering it as it has done to so many, many lagoons. It has been helped materially here by the long fences of bamboo stakes which the villagers have built across the lagoon for fastening their fish traps. Floating grasses become caught in these fences and soon take root, rapidly growing into yet another barrier across the water. When the new grasses make fish traps there useless the villagers in canoes simply drive in a new fence elsewhere, too lazy to pull up the old and thus at least partly protect the lagoon that feeds them. Why should they pull up those overgrown fences, they ask, when there is plenty of water everywhere?

While the P.O. holds court you climb up into the House Tamboran and are immediately interested in pillows of wood in the cubicles, and many fantastic stools. The pillows are made to fit under the neck, carved out of solid blocks about six inches high, stools and pillows well carved with representations of crocodiles and pigs, dogs, birds, and half-man, half-fish or animal designs.

Well away from the House Tamboran, and you are followed by the belles of the village, your every movement closely watched an eagerly commented upon. There is not the slightest thing that their bright eyes miss, no slightest incident that their eager serpents' tongues fail to avidly wag about. Some of these brown beauties wear their heads quite shaven, others with a close crop, others under a mop of tiny ringlets, yet others are bobbed. This is a comparatively new fashion in Sydney, you remember with surprise, yet it is old stuff to these prehistoric swamp maidens.

The curiosity of these lively Eves in practically every village you've stayed at has on occasion been embarrassing in the extreme. Every action, no matter what it is, of the mysterious white man is of the most intense interest to these "sticky-beaking" eyes.

You've learnt it is quite useless to sneak craftily away into the grass when you feel inclined, for there are always bright eyes peering at you from amongst the grasses, gasps and giggles and "ohs" from unseen women and children. And you simply cannot hide behind a tree, you'd never dreamt it before but you just can't - because there are eyes all around the tree!

In your most luscious moments you've never dreamt you could ever be so infernally embarrassed by the fair sex.

28

AUSTRALIA'S BURDEN

ONCE again steaming up the brown stream, now growing narrower, you land on the bank to walk to Kangannaman village, a beautiful walk. Not even the whisper of your footsteps upon the carpeted leaves. Foliaged trees meet overhead, just here and there allowing shafts of sunlight that paint the vegetation a soft green. The air scented by Nature at its kindest, the happy trilling of birds. You are sorry, then amazed, when you step out into brilliant sunlight and a majestic House Tamboran strikes your sight like a slap in the face. It stands in a clearing where the grass is like a lawn, its towering, peaked gables rising grandly above the tallest trees. It is a shock, this barbaric, beautifully constructed, massive building set in the heart of a New Guinea swamp, erected by savages using Stone Age tools, mostly the stone axe and adze. You stand in admiration, wondering and wondering. Whence did they learn the expert engineering knowledge at least of leverage and pulleys necessary to raise and lift those great beams into position-beams that were the trunks of trees? And for ropes they would only have those they fashioned out of vines and cane. Yet here firmly stands a massive work wonderful in its conception, perfect in completion, a miracle of native craftsmanship. And all your life you had thought the life of a swamp was just a few wild ducks and smell of water-sodden reeds.

You walk slowly on until close enough to admire the fantastic carvings adorning the great posts and beams. This is a real culture, doomed to extinction, you regretfully remember, by the advance of civilization. For in controlled districts you have seen that the "present day" native, with all the advantages of modem tools, cannot execute work to compare with that of his father who only had the crudest of native stone implements to hand.

You glance away up. High in those gables, and again set within apertures in the towering walls, there grin down upon you numerous skulls. You try to count how many poor devils have been butchered to decorate this great House Tamboran, but the building is so big and so high, there are so many hidden nooks on all sides that finally you give up, while the skulls just grin down.

You climb up, and step into the great, gloomy hall. You try to distinguish the carvings - there are far too many. Plenty of stools, all encircling the smouldering fires on the hard-baked clay floor. On benches thick-caked with grease from the oil-smeared bodies of past and present savages await wooden pillows and neck-rests in numerous designs of crawling tortoise, writhing crocodile and snapping dog. Enormous masks, some almost man-size glare in frightening designs from the walls. One dingy, colour-splashed cubicle appears to be the "paint room", some colours ready mixed on clay "plates" and pots. Yellows extracted from the roots of a bush, reds extracted from a tree, various colours from clays, lime, and mineral oxides. Weapons seem to be everywhere. Overhead, huge beams twelve to fifteen inches in diameter span the building. Far overhead the roof is lost in gloom, but as you peer here and there you see the shadowy white of skulls. You could spend slow days in this Place of Spirits, and still find things.

The strong floor is of split Limbon palm. Here lie in hidden stores all the sacred masks, fanciful regalia and paints, musical and other instruments used in "sing-sings" and initiation ceremonies.

Should a woman see the hidden things in the house of mysteries she will surely die. And so firmly implanted is this superstition that no woman dare look within the House Tamboran, House of the Spirits. You are sceptical that even fear of death halts the curiosity of the women. But believe me, they are scared.

Out in the blessed sunlight again, you wander through the village while the P.O. makes his trip of inspection with the Luluai and tul-tul, seeing that the D.O's last orders as left in the Book Kiap have been carried out. A large village, large houses, too, raising their muratta-covered roofs high amid the clusters of coconut and betel-nut and palm, with, in lighter contrast the kapiak-trees, lou-lou and banana growing in wild luxuriance, hibiscus and croton adding vivid colour. Well-carved ladder poles give access to the houses, a reversed pole indicates that the owners are not at home. Numerous sleeping baskets like mammoth caterpillars ten to fifteen feet long and two feet high lie in disorderly array on the Limbon floors, just as the sleepers had crawled out of them, reminding you of the family bedrooms when the yawning family have crawled out for breakfast. Fires smoulder on hearths of clay, the smoke rising lazily up to cane baskets shaped much like dovecots, in which fish of all sizes lie curing. On the clay fireplace soup in clay pots is simmering. Earthenware pots, two and three feet high and from one to two feet in diameter, all painted in intricate designs, are lined along the outer walls, all stored with sac-sac. Numerous spears, heavily barbed and mostly bamboo-pointed, with other grisly weapons, lie in handy racks above the sleeping baskets. Curiously, you note that these weapons, generally so well cared for, have taken on a coat of smoke-blackened grime through very recent disuse. So swiftly is the law of the white man corning into this troubled land. The heads of dead relatives, modelled in clay to a perfect likeness, even to the hair, keep silent watch over all.

Outside, brown-skinned children in laughing nakedness play in the warm sunshine upon the close grass. A wealth of shell necklaces and armlets emphasize their glistening skin as yet untouched by tribal markings. Their chubby legs look like bending under the weight of their little pot bellies. This may be, is, a world of swamps, but there is abundant food for all here. The youngsters scurry like bushrats at your approach, peering out from the shelter of their mother's pul-pul, their large, beautiful eyes all curious timidity as they cling to the fluffy grass skirt, quite oblivious to the fine glimpse of shapely leg thus betrayed.

Long-snouted pigs, recently household pets that in their infancy shared the common sleeping baskets with the family, now grunt disconsolately outside the strongly constructed fence enclosing the village. They must now sleep, if sleep be possible, with the mosquitoes in the long grass outside the fence - although their thick hide, mud-covered, should be ample protection. What the natives gain is clear evidence in their healthy skins and clean bodies.

You could dawdle a long time in a village such as this, but the duties of the P.O. keep the pinnace ever moving on upstream. Across on the bank the P.O. points to coconut and betel-nut palms towering above dense undergrowth. You expect to see another village, and know why not when you land. For creepers hang in profusion from bleached and carved posts which once supported large houses. Riot of shrubs and grasses has completely taken over the once fine village of Yentjan. Continued raids by the powerful people of Parambi at last drove the survivors from their village.

You follow the P.O. and his Native Police along a foot-wide track hugging the jungle-clad bank of a deep, black creek. On through a thick belt of jungle and you emerge out onto a sunlit kuni-grass plain, stretching miles away. Up in the branches of trees overhead still hang heaps of flotsam, ominous proof of the floods that turn these grass plains into a sea at least fifty miles wide. You have lost all idea of proportion now so far as swamps are concerned, for swampy happenings and swampy things are on such a vast scale here.

An hour's walk across that sea of kuni and you come to a narrow neck of swamp bridged by a log. In defence, how easy to tip that log into the swamp! You cross the bridge and see the House Tamboran of the new village of Yentjan amidst its tropical trees. You approach, to catch a glimpse of savages fleeing for the bush. Myriad mosquitoes make you still less pleased at this scurvy welcome. You carny on towards the backs of houses lying deep in the bush, but only catch a glimpse of the naked legs of men fleeing into the long grass, the flying pul-pul of a woman as she vanishes. The shouts of your interpreters notifying the fleeing ones of your peaceful intentions echo through the bush.

Into silence.

The P.O. shrugs, orders his boys to try to make contact at least with some of the villagers, then turns towards the House Kiap, Quietly you think that if your parents, and you too for as long as you could remember, had existed in daily fear of headhunters then you, too, would fly at a shadow.

A glance at the Village Book shows that the census for this village has been but recently taken, and that difficulty had been experienced in inducing the villagers to "line" - that is, to become approachable, to be counted. You saw that for yourself in those flying legs. You wonder how the D.O. made "contact" in the first place. Grimly the P.O. points to all the neatly phrased instructions the D.O. has written in the Village Book. You do not envy the D.O. his job in seeing those instructions are carried out. He, and the P.O. also, is welcome to all the honour and glory and pioneering and the Brotherhood of Man touch for yours. Mentally you think if those natives wish to stick to their pigs and mud and mosquitoes you for one will never trouble them again.

Still in its natural state, the village smells like a pigsty. Pigs wallowing at will in the filthy mud beneath the houses which are surrounded by the forest of mosquito-breeding grass, the narrow tracks ankle deep in mud and filth. Even in broad daylight mosquitoes swarm in countless numbers. Yet again you wonder how on earth that tiny handful of white men spread over such a vast area finally get the hundreds and hundreds of villages such as this under control, and clean and healthy.

You battle your way back through that grass forest, in heartfelt relief reaching the pinnace, the open river, and the ammonia bottle.

As the pinnace chugs again up stream what pleasure it is to breathe the free, open air, to gaze at the sky because it is so clean and vast and unencumbered of anything. But your freedom from enclosing, at times almost suffocating, irritations is not for long. The pinnace turns to cross the river then cautiously noses into a narrow barrad (channel) barely visible in the gigantic pitpit growing up from the water. Just up on the banks overgrown sugarcane fights to push its leaves up towards the sky. Yam foliage supported by ten-foot high stakes grows profusely in neat gardens upon either bank. Again you marvel at the growing capacity of this vast swamp land.

Slowly the pinnace pushes aside the protesting and overhanging grasses which rustle in one massed sighing. The sense of power in all that grass is frightening; at times when deep within these grass forests you feel that such a feeble, tenacious thing might be capable of choking up all the lands of the earth.

The boat's crew stand fore and aft, expert brown arms handling long bamboo poles, alternately testing the depth then pushing with muscle and weight of chest to help force the pinnace round the bends against the sighing grass, reedy grass now, arching overhead. Soon, the propeller chokes with grass, under water you see it as a deep, confused mass of hair-like roots. The pinnace is forced to a dragging stop. You light your pipes, then pick up rifles and lean overside to keep a sharp watch while the boss boy slides over into the crocodile infested water and frees the propeller. Then on again, only to be pulled up again, so slowly, so definitely. Comes a halt when the propeller is choked with rope-like reeds knotted round it into a tight ball, necessitating vigorous slashes with a knife.

Laboriously the pinnace pushes ahead. Myriads of ants and insects are shaken off the swaying pit-pit grass and drop down upon the pinnace and you. This continuous insect rain keeps falling into eyes, nostrils, ears, down your neck, into your clothing and proceeds to give you irritating hell. All sorts of things can happen to you in the life of a swamp, but you have ceased to care, you long to get out of it.

You believe me now that there are swamps and swamps. The harsh boom of some hidden garramut warns you these are not the swamps of Aussieland.

29

WITHIN THE WORLD OF THE SWAMP MEN

AT last the pinnace pushes through into an open lagoon. You whip up the rifles and fire at three crocodiles splashing off floating logs down into grass-entangled depths. At the startling report, wildfowl in screeching clouds rise skyward, their wings disturbing the heavy air to waft a sweet, exotic scent over all, while lotus and other small, long-legged birds run in squeaking alarm over the huge water-lily leaves that carpet the water away out into distance. The lagoon is narrow, but long, its end vanishing into grasses. The pinnace must slowly push its way through the huge circular leaves, three and four feet wide, that carpet the water like a ballroom floor massed with great pink and white and blue flowers in a blaze of colour. Then before you stretches a seemingly impenetrable wall of pit-pit grass. But the guide swings the pinnace sharply into a passage quite invisible until the bow pushes aside the grass, which in a whispering rustle immediately closes around the pinnace. You are swallowed in grass again, it meets even over the top of the pinnace, pressing in rustling urgency against the vessel's sides, where its swaying fronds surge inboard to kiss the leaves swaying in from over the opposite gunwale. You seem hopelessly lost, deep within a sea of grass. Grimly you wonder just how you could ever get out of this frightful environment if your crew boys were to suddenly dive overside and' abandon you. It is with genuine relief that you feel the pinnace suddenly surge forward to shoot out into a clear stream. Under the lovely sky again, and you see the wee village of Yogono right ahead, a Walt Disney village with its quaint little houses poked high up on stilts. But now a huge log bars the way-this precautionary defence gives the villages time to scamper away into the grass. The united efforts of the launch crew finally displace the log, then slowly the pinnace forges past Yogono. Eventually the narrow stream widens under a canopy of majestic trees whose tops meet overhead to break the sunlight into dancing shafts of light.

Sacrilege comes in a paralysing roar of sound echoed by two soft thumps as two plump pigeons strike the pinnace edge and splash into the water. The echoing roll of the shotgun report turns into a bedlam of screeching cockatoos and parrots as pigeons in waves of colour swish agitatedly overhead.

Again the pinnace turns a right-angled bend and gradually leaves, behind those beautiful trees, the stream narrowing again under the vicious encroachment of that everlasting pit-pit grass. And now well-kept native gardens of yam, sugarcane, and tobacco in profusion appear on the banks.

Suddenly the pinnace rises precipitately with a long, choking sigh. At the soft bump you snatch for a hold, hardly breathing as gear gently slides overboard. The pinnace sheers over sharply -you stare at one another as your feet feel the heavy, soggy thing below-then she slides safely forward and rights herself. If that log had punched a hole in her bottom you would have been left wallowing in a truly nasty fix.

Soon afterward the pinnace pushes through into yet another lagoon, again encircled by wheeling clouds of duck and osprey, cloud after cloud of waterfowl settling ever and again just ahead. Fortunately, you had fired no shot here, which is why the snub nose of a canoe emerged like a gigantic crocodile from the grass wall fronting you. The women and youngsters aboard stared a second, then the water Hew from their broad-bladed paddles as they wheeled and vanished back into the channel from which they had come. You laugh heartily at their amazed surprise and frenzied retreat, but the P.O. has instantly ordered the pinnace to follow them. The grass in that winding, pit-pit lined barrad soon slackens the launch, you never catch even a glimpse of that long canoe again. You are quietened at the thought that Stone Age savages - and women, too, at that - in a Stone Age dug-out have here this day easily and convincingly defeated the most modern "water machinery" of civilized man. Eventually the barrad leads the pinnace out on to a large lake, a wonderful sight set deep within that sea of grass. Had you ever imagined a real lake within a swamp? The relief of the great open sky, of an unobstructed sheet of water glistening into distance-you feel what a joy it is to really breathe freely, almost certainly for the first time in your life you realize fully what a delight is space and distance. Away on the farthest shore are just visible the tall house-tops of Malangei village. Three miles to the left, like a dark, indistinct cloud, is the line of trees near Parambei. Six crocodiles sunbathing quietly submerge before the launch. Scattered over the lake drift large dug-outs filled with brown-skinned women and children tending fish traps and lines. A shrill, warning cry screeches urgently out over the water, the canoes in dozens race away to converge towards their respective villages. The crew boys grin, the P.O. looks solemn as soon you are left in solitary possession of the lake, forced to wend your way through innumerable tufts of grasses anchored to stakes where fishing traps are set.

Across the great lake from Parambei now floats the boom of a garramut, quickly echoed from Malangei. The P.O. swings the pinnace head towards Parambei. The noise increases while the booming grows to be sullenly echoed and re-echoed across the lake, the air now reverberating as the giant garramuts boom through the drumming of their lesser brethren. There is no laughter now from the crew boys. Uneasily you notice a grimness on the faces of the Native Police as the pinnace forges steadily ahead into that sea of sound. She negotiates a tortuous passage that winds through waving grasses, past floating islands that have grounded with the falling of the waters. For this is a lake on which islands float, gliding away to touch of wind and perhaps draw of distant river tide. Prettily, imperceptibly by day. By night, barely gliding past, or looming up apparently soft as a drifting black cloud-dangerous shadows of the night.

The launch edges round an especially large island, which to you appears properly anchored. As finally you come in round it you sail into such a thunderous boom of garramuts you hardly notice the relief of perfectly clear water at last. On the shore ahead many great houses stand high, people swarming everywhere, roar of chanting voices. Scores of well-made canoes are tethered to floating logs, scores more are drawn up on the shelving shore of Parambei. There is so much to see, but you notice especially a curious, long, efficient bridge of logs supported on crossed poles. This bridge has handrails of bamboo and spans the water right across from the shore to the anchored island. These savages of the great grass lake have the intelligence to plan and do things. But the pinnace is steadily heading in towards shore, you see the P.O. is determined to land; despite yourself your hand stealthily feels for the reassuring touch of the automatic, though you know it will be hopeless if something really happens. You are now steaming into a veritable thunder of sound from the pounding of the giant and the lesser garramuts, intensified by the kunda drums, the shrilling of the long and short bamboo flutes, the angry whine of innumerable bull-roarers, roar of voices. A mad riot of indescribable sound to your throbbing ear drums, fit music to these savage surroundings.

You land in an atmosphere of tense savagery, the keyed-up emotions of these superstitious people wound up to concert pitch. With considerable relief you learn that the savagely hostile atmosphere is but partly towards you. For a sing-sing which has gone on for two days and nights is at its height. The arrival of the patrol is but an unwelcome event which these he-men are determined shall not interfere with their business. However, the P.O. is just as determined to meet the unwilling Luluai and discuss the business of his visit. You watch the quiet preparations of the P.O., the steadiness of his Police Boys, the efficiency and firmness with which this tiny patrol is going to carry out its job in the midst of blood-lusting thousands already worked up to primitive hysteria.

You are only a looker-on with the patrol, just a lucky meeting has given you a chance to see life in this vast Swamp Land which you would never have seen, never have known existed otherwise. You glance around at the heaving squads of dancers, at the sullen, athletic beaters of the garramuts, the hurrying life from the shore to the village. Big savages, broad chests panting with excitement, eyes animal bright, taking not even a scowling glance at the patrol as you move towards the centre of the ceremonies. Savages decked in magnificent headdresses of bird of paradise, osprey plumes swaying as they dance, clinking of shell ornaments round chests and big, sweating limbs. You notice that many a brave flaunts that ominous loin covering - the flying-fox skin! Each so clad proudly clenches his kum-bung (lime) container, from the long serrated stick of which hang finely plaited chains of grass with swaying tassels of vivid feathers. You count eight swinging from one great brute's kum-bung stick - he scowls in a majestic aloofness, this killer who has taken eight heads.

An incessant stream of befeathered warriors is moving in and out of a huge bannis (fence) completely hiding from view a large House Tamboran wherein the young men of the village are undergoing initiation. The whole great place rings with an incessant crash upon crash of sound from native cymbals.

Well, you are in the heart of a swamp world now with a vengeance. And just what are you going to do about it!

30

WHERE ISLANDS FLOAT

FIRMLY, methodically, and understandingly, the P.O. carries on with his duties. Then you take up quarters in the central House Tamboran for the night; this particular house is not being used. It is going to be a wild night, judging by the fearful muffled row coming from what sounds the distant outside. But in this great shadowy place all seems puzzlingly quiet but for booming echoes. You are curious to explore the half-glimpsed things in this gloomy cavern, but the P.O. has only time for a quick inspection of the village. He will not be able to do much because of the excitement and he wisely does not desire to interfere with the ceremonies. But he is going to put on a "show" all the same, and once again you find your way outside, strolling past the dancing groups and squads down along the village.

These Parambei houses are exceptionally large, measuring from eighty to a hundred feet long by thirty to fifty feet wide. They stand high on piles which are now leaning, bowed down by the passing of time, blackened and browned with age and smoke and grime. Successive generations of tribesmen have been well sheltered beneath these thick, muratta-thatched roofs. But it is now obvious that they must eventually go under beneath the terrific tropical storms, the yearly sea of floods, and the ravages of white ants. Against such odds, the marvel is that they have weathered the elements so long, proof of the sturdy cunning of the long-dead native builders. And they built these great places with the help only of Stone Age tools.

Stepping under a big house, curious as to the method of building, you leap aside and yell, staring down at the hideous jowl of a crocodile - you had almost put your foot upon him. As you leap back you are astonished to see he is securely lashed to an upright. Yes, and there are two others, their slits of eyes coldly upon you. In one of those foolish urges that come upon man at times you pick up a pole and jab the fellow you almost trod on. The pole is dashed from your hands by a furious swirl of the tail, you leap out from under, followed by a yap-like snarl.

Yes, you've got the shivers and serve you right, for though you know now that those crocodiles are neither dead nor asleep. They are very much alive, and very angry.

You find that under every house others are securely tied up, scores and scores and scores of them, of all sizes from babies two and three feet long to slimy man-eaters of ten and fifteen powerful feet. You feel savagely glad-a touch of the primitive rising in you also-that all these hideous brutes are to be killed and eaten. They are but part of the enormous supply of food gathered together for consumption during this prolonged sing-sing. The flesh of the puk-puk (crocodile) is preferred here by the tribesmen even to wild pig. A boy who could talk pidgin would lick his lips and express his taste this way: "Good feller arbush too much!" -probably patting his bingy while grinning hugely.

The hurrying people still take no notice of you. Groups are eating, groups are dancing, others staggering under loads of food, others solemnly painting and dressing in their befeathered finery. You come on to a long native road behind the houses; it is like a clearing bordering the edge of thick bush, and carries on past the entire length of the village and on to Malangei village a mile distant. In this big village there is more than one House Tamboran; each belongs to a different section or group within the village. They are built a hundred yards or so apart, standing end to end, raising their high, peaked gables above the coconut palms.

Away along each side of the clearing are what were once great earth mounds where the people sat to watch and applaud now long-forgotten rites and orgies. All are thickly lined with towering palms. Elsewhere also is mute evidence that this big village has survived throughout a long, long history. Probably it was a thriving, fightable village when the Druids were building their mounds and sacred stones at Stonehenge.

You see that in the centre of the clearing, a few yards' distance from the ends of each House Tamboran, stand "fingers" in slabs of stone three and four feet high encircling mounds some ten feet in diameter, riveted by timbers. Herein flourish a profusion of trees and shrubs. The riveting is fast falling to decay; green moss is covering the blackened stones; you stand a moment wondering what long-forgotten cult was this that has left its last lingering footprint in the moving path of time.

But now, through the Luluai, comes a half-defiant, surlily gracious invitation. The White Man party will be now allowed a glimpse at the ceremonies. Not the real ceremonies, of course, no white man living will ever be allowed to see those - so you are given to understand. But while the actors are preparing for the next serious phase of the routine you will be allowed a peep, a "look-see".

Thus you are permitted to pass through the tall fence screening the great House Tamboran in which the initiation ceremonies are taking place. Passing the gauntlet of those many savage, staring faces as you approach the great building you are thrilled with curiosity, but feel that your automatic is handy, for all that.

Inside that huge, gloomy place you cannot move about, you half glimpse countless intriguing things, but you just have to do as you are told, or rather as you are frowned and grunted and pointed at-merely stand politely aside and watch and be quiet. Not that you could make any noise in the noise which is soon to be. It is plainly indicated to you also that others will make all the noise. And they do.

Two star actors advance to do their turn clothed in fearsome masks fitting over head and shoulders. From these masks hang "weeping" shrouds of vividly dyed grasses completely covering the swaying bodies to the knees, the giant garramuts boom, the lesser garramuts join in as the kunda drums reverberate, the cymbals clash and your ear-drums go "Bang! Bang! Bang!"

The performers posture and preen themselves in the queerest of attitudes, all of which holds meaning to the hundreds of eyes staring through the gloom, whilst from under their masks the dancers' bamboo flutes, pitched in a high and low key, screech and whistle the weirdest of questioning and answering calls. Those strangely "talking" sounds are very impressive if only you could understand the "language".

Close by now come two highly painted men in magnificent bird of paradise headdresses, wearing broad, highly ornamental belts, from the rear of which stand cocked up brilliant tufts of grass and feathers for all the world like the highly spectacular tail of some prized rooster. These men perform on six-foot long bamboo flutes set in different keys and wailing a barbaric music to which their bodies keep time by stiffly bending and straightening at the knees, a weird effect accentuated by the jerking time kept by each man's "tail".

Without an instant's cessation the "fighting" of the lesser and giant garramuts reverberate through the walls and far away out over lake and swamps, not one beat from any drum being lost, one performer relieving another and taking the sticks before the player had released his hands.

Numerous queerly bedecked natives manipulating varying lengths of bamboo wail and whine and whistle and roar their quota of "music"; some phases of it remind you of a busy day at the cattle yards where hundreds of calves are blaring for their mothers answered by frantic mooing. On richly carved stools of varied designs, around small fires inside this great place, squat a betel-nut-chewing crowd occupying every inch of space, each man painted and oil-smeared, each adding to the sweating, foetid atmosphere, while ever and again they work their long, serrated kum-bung sticks in and out of their containers, producing with studied effect a rasping rattle. Through what your deafened ears can absorb, the shadow pictures you can see comes a tantalizing query of memory-locusts! How do they make that queer, shrill sound? Is it by the drawing backwards and forwards of the serrated edges of their hind legs? Have these squatting buddas copied the locusts with their serrated lime sticks? Decorating a long rack along one giant wall hang the tambus of the initiates undergoing initiation, wonderfully carved wooden faces, masks having the nose grotesquely extended down over the mouth to terminate in the bill of a duck, the snout of a crocodile or pig, or the nose of a dog, the cheeks and chins artistically decorated with tiny shells inlaid into the wood.

Time simply flies by until suddenly aware you are more or less politely motioned, "Now clear out of this!"

Greatly you would have liked to witness at least some of the secret rites; the devil dancers are coming, and dances of the sorcerers, and the dances of the spirits. As well cry for the moon. You make for your own House Tamboran, amazed to see that evening has come. You sleep but fitfully, for outside the crowds of excited humanity keep sing-sing going all night without a moment's cessation.

Next morning the garramuts are still booming, the P.O. is up betimes, for duty calls. You are just about to leave this big, gloomy sleeping place when some queer shape attracts your attention over near the shadowy end.

It is a big, throne-like chair hewn out of a solid log. This chair thing is some five feet high and three feet in diameter. Carved upon its back is a wonderfully proportioned and coloured face, two feet wide. The seat is supported above the base by four well-carved figures. You wish for the time to examine this thing minutely, for the knowledge to question what it means. But the P.O. shrugs, he is pressed for time and must be moving. All that has unwillingly been told him is a legend. It is that if this seat is ever destroyed, or disposed of, then the village of Parambei will completely "finish".

31
SURPRISES OF THE SWAMP LANDS

THE P.O. orders the boss boy take the launch on ahead. He must walk across to Malangei to "see what's doing" on the way. You walk under a delightful avenue of breadfruit-trees, then over a plain of waving grass stretching far away. "All correct!" at Malangei village and you are aboard the pinnace again, steaming across a short bend of the lake, thankful the thunder of the garramuts is no longer pounding in your ears but merely rolling across the lake. The pinnace enters a narrow channel that has been cut through the tall grass of a swamp, the water soon is exceptionally deep, grasses stretch far as the eye can see in every direction, all that is the world here is water and grasses and sky.

Presently the pinnace is nosing into another well-defined channel fifty feet wide, heavily infested with crocodiles. Then soon you exclaim at a most welcome sight away to the left-the hills of Aibon and Chambri, as distinct landmarks amidst that sea of grass as the Pyramids are in the desert.

The stream runs nearly parallel to those hills - you can hardly keep your eyes off them-for some miles, occasionally the pinnace must detour round floating islands. You come out on to the great lake of Chambri, with Chambri mountain ten miles away rising right up out of the lake.

A wonderful sight that lake and mount, and the P.O. assures you that as yet very few white men indeed have ever seen it. The lake stretches away to a dim horizon of grass. Big islands float out there, their trees alive with birds. In far distance, that ever-intriguing distance towards which you wish to go, beckons the hazy outline of real mountains. And yet, strangely, maybe because of some queer characteristic of light upon this sea of water and grass, you can clearly see columns of smoke arising from villages far away up there, villages not yet visited by white men. Once again, how different a scene from your previous idea of a swamp!

You feel this weird country is entrancing as you gaze towards those mysterious jungle-clad mountains, mighty range upon range, peopled by - what? This can be a dangerous country, it stirs some deep, primal instinct within the civilized man-there is danger here that he might corne to stay.

Eagerly you gaze towards Chambri swiftly growing, you are glad that the P.O's duty for some reason bids him climb it. You land, he sets the boys to cutting a track up the hill. It proves a strenuous climb, though well rewarded by the magnificent view of lake and grass and mountains.

The P.O's mapping duty done, you return to the pinnace to cross the lake, and eventually find your way back to the Sepik. Before reaching the river, though, you find that even in that short time several of the narrow swamp channels through which the pinnace had laboriously poked her way have been blocked by grass, which again and yet again mean a tiresome waiting time until the boys can cut a passage wide and deep enough to pole the pinnace through. For the hundredth time you are glad of the guides; it would be awful to find yourself hopelessly hemmed in by this terrifying sea of grasses.

And the crocodiles. And the vastness.

And the loneliness - where invisible eyes might be glaring at you but a few yards away.

And the mosquitoes!

What a relief to be out on the open river again. You camp a night. There are uncountable millions of tons of grass out there.

But that grass "gets" a man. Tucked in under the net, you think and think of it in the long, mosquito-ridden "silence" of the night. There are uncountable billions of tons of grass out there. Maybe, some day, those thousands of square miles of country will be drained. Machines will mow down the forests of grass in thousands of tons per day. Perhaps it could be turned into pulp to help supply the newspapers of the world. And at long last, when the long job is done, what limitless plains of the finest agricultural land in the world would be laid open for the farmer! The Valley of the Nile would be but the merest creek would not be a creek by comparison.

Only a dream, of course, but then perhaps the whole world was made on a dream.

Korogo is pleasing, for it is a large, clean, well-kept village.

Fowls cost one shilling each. But from Korogo you "go grass" again. The P.O. must visit a swamp village only just being brought under control. You walk along a native pad ankle-deep in mud to an extensive lagoon, almost a lake. Hefty villagers are carrying light canoes along behind you. You launch these, and are paddled across the lagoon. Then you walk in earnest along a barely discernible pad through dense bush cluttered with battalions of creepers struggling against the trees for a glimpse of the life-giving sun. From that struggle of Nature you step into a gloomier, deathly quiet fight that encompasses you with a feeling of what life must have been like in the primal ages-the sour, stagnant gloom of a sac-sac swamp. Presently, none but a born swamp-man could keep any sense of direction. The mud deepens, you drag out each foot loaded with clinging grey mud that sucks back with choking sigh. Great knotted cables trail down from motionless palms whose grey trunks are scabby with decaying mosses. Thankfully you trudge on into gloom-laden bush again, but not for long. You squelch into another sac-sac swamp again and soon all sign of a track vanishes under russet-stained water. You grow fearful of taking a false step, closely now you watch the back, the movements of the P.O., who is closely following the movements of the guide in front. That guide is now probing for every foot of the way with his submerged feet. Uneasily you realize there is no telling what depth of mud and filthy water lies just to the left and right of whatever he is probing for. Soon, you are wading with Blondin delicacy, realizing there is some sort of log work under the mud that your feet must grope for. Vegetation-stained water is now up to your waist, your body slowly brushes aside the rotting sac-sac fronds partly submerged in the still, filthy water. Your foot definitely touches a log and a chill shoots up your spine - is it a crocodile? But the others are slowly, cautiously floundering on. In heartfelt relief you think, "Perhaps there are no crocodiles here!" Surely even a crocodile could not see in this black, beastly water, thick with sediment of decayed vegetation. And yes, of course, fish would never live *here*!

You are really following, your feet groping for, a native defence road. You begin to realize, to "feelingly appreciate", how wonderfully skilful these swamp savages are in the matter of defence -they have to be. Otherwise their fathers' fathers would have all lost their heads long, long ago. At this particular period of your visit you see that in no land in the world is that eternal rule so grimly stressed-e"the survival of the fittest, of the ever prepared".

Under your feet has actually been built up-with what labour and skill, all by help of the stone-headed adze! - a narrow track, a long line of logs not actually laid end to end, but staggered, so that when you so very cautiously step along to the end of one you have to grope by foot for the beginning of the next. On either side lie deep water and mud. Enemies, to reach the distant village, must know the secret of that long line of logs running under the discoloured water across the bottom of the swamp though such a swamp appears to have no real bottom. And then, if it were betrayed, or even if enemies did find it, it could be so easily defended. Invaders could not rely alone on canoes, which are impracticable in such a swamp.

Presently you are slowly dragging yourself through that beastly swamp with the slimy, foul-smelling water up to your chest, thoroughly convinced that all the heads in New Guinea are not worth the experience. Occasionally you are right down to your neck, painfully, laboriously groping ahead with one leg and foot for some mud-encased log a step ahead before. you dare move the other foot. Under such ideal conditions the mosquitoes are giving you, all of you, pure, unadulterated hell.

You go through three hours of this, alternate stretches of bush, mud, sac-sac swamp and water before at last sighting the outer barricade of the village of Chauash, catching a flying glimpse of two women disappearing through the tall barricade. No mere woman, you feel, was worth that wretched trip, let alone a naked "swamp rat".

The barricade gate is definitely closed against you. After a noisy harangue by the interpreter, answered surlily from inside, a small opening grudgingly appears. In single file you go cautiously through, your spine creeping lest a club come smashing down upon your head. The boat's crew bodyguard are intensely alert, you forget your late trip and are keyed up for fight as you step through.

A quick glance shows a cleared space set amidst impassable undergrowth, while fifty yards ahead another strong barricade effectively bars the way. Away farther back housetops seem peering over the barricade. Your party stands there, peering, listening-all is deathly silence.

The P.O. advances, you follow him up to the second barricade.

And here it takes long-continued eloquence before a narrow hole appears and you are allowed creep through.

Every soul except three have made their get-away. These three stand back with both alarm and a dubiously friendly smile on anxious faces, prepared to make friends, prepared to fly. The P.O. through the interpreter soon makes them feel at ease. Soon they smile and expand their chests, they really are quite civilized men, they explain, and great travellers. One had even been for a little time a Police Boy, or "attached" to some patrol, while the other two are time-expired plantation labourers.

One day, "long time ago", while on a trading visit to Malangei village, a wandering recruiter had come up river. In a great spirit of adventure, unable to resist the marvellous presents, they had signed on for a term of labour "far away" down by the river mouth. Their term expired they had returned to their village, but quickly "gone native" again. You all are glad they had not quite forgotten all about the white man and his ways, else those barricades would never have been opened. It was through these three same natives that the D.O. but a short time before had been able to make his first contact with the village, the first contact that can mean so much.

Chauash literally means "bush natives", or "men of the bush", which means "wild men" from any sophisticated natives' viewpoint. Thus the Australian aboriginal, if he is a Kimberley native and now a "station boy", will contemptuously .refer to the wild natives in the ranges as "munjons". In other Australian areas the term generally is "myalls". Thus the villagers when brought under control on the Sepik referred to their headhunting brothers as chauash, "wild bushmen".

You can give no opinion, for all you have seen of these people was the fleeing stern of a woman. As the P.O. makes his inspection he remarks, "We cannot strictly class these people as 'swamp men', for we have found no canoes - unless they have them hidden away out in the bush somewhere. But by the looks of it these people are simply chauash."

You climb gingerly up into the House Tamboran, grimly reassured that in the outside silence the scared boat's crew are keeping a sharp look-out against surprise. Cautious against ambush yourself in this gloomy place, you explore the upper floor of that temple of horrors. Two rows of giant garramuts lie there, grotesquely, but splendidly carved, even you can now recognize that here is a change of culture quite different from the river natives. All around the place the giant masks, the beams and sacred objects are so rich in paintings and barbaric decorations that the interest really repays you for that awful walk through the mud of ages. As you peer about, ever finding new things, you become aware of numerous skulls sneering down at you from many shadowy portholes. So that these chauash, hunted in turn yet smaller fry. There is ample evidence also that at least up to a matter of only months ago these elusive people have played merry hell within the security of this barricaded fastness.

The P.O. is searching for, finds, the Village Book, the "Book Kiap". You come to see it in almost as much curiosity as you have peered into those forbidden cubicles. A civilized, solid sort of ledger book in this hotbed of savagery! You wonder at the fearful superstition that has caused it to be left alone. You wonder more that one isolated white man, for company only his own adventurous spirit, devotion to duty, and half a dozen badly scared Police Boys, should succeed in venturing into such a place alone. And make contact. And actually issue orders to these highly explosive, dumbfounded savages.

You wonder that he ever expects such orders to be carried out.

You wonder again how he ever got away with it, however he got back to the river alive.

And yet, such things have happened again and again, to village after village as the White Man's Law spreads slowly but so very surely ever farther back into all the forbidding chauash country.

The same has happened, years and years ago, over the great mountains in adjoining Papua, but most of us in Australia, let alone the world, have never been aware of it. The same is happening today, only with incomparably greater organization, supply, and security.

The D.O. had come across this village when away from Headquarters investigating some particularly murderous spearing affray.

As the P.O. reads the few notes that begin this book, you peer at the page. You note that the D.O. has left instructions for the Luluai and the villagers, and for the guidance of the P.O. who visits in his footsteps, that headhunting must immediately cease, also plain murder, the village must be immediately cleaned up, pigs chased outside, grass cut to keep down the mosquitoes, a census of every man, woman and child taken, etc., etc., etc. and you break into a smile at the cheek of it all, and glance up at the skulls grinning down. But there is a last note that demands also that a firm roadway, above water and mud, shall be built right away back across that awful swamp.

This seems too rich. You don't express your opinion as to what hope you believe the D.O. has of ever seeing his bridge building instructions ever carried out, but you do wish he'd "controlled" the village and left those instructions a year or two earlier at least. Very uneasily you remember that frightful track under the swamp - you'd forgotten all about it under the sense of menace and intense interest of the last two hours.

The P.O. adds a few notes to the book, frowning, worried at his lack of contact with the natives, the work to be done here.

It is refreshing to stroll outside into partial sunlight. The P.O. leads the way to the back of the village, intent on yet another effort to make further contact with the villagers. But over the palisade there is no track leading back into the wild bush, it had been allowed long since to grow completely over as a further aid against attack and also to baffle pursuers should it become necessary to fly

The P.O. wishes to advance and have a try, but the frightened guide instantly whimpers alarm, earnestly assuring us that by now out there "plenty men of the bush" have joined the Villagers and that these men of the bush "savvy plenty fella fight"! In fact, they appear to be "hogging" for it. The three natives who opened the barricade volubly back him up, you can see they are in earnest, can easily guess, too, that should you cross over the barricade they will simply vanish in the bush. The crew boys hang on the interpreter's words and the P.O's decision. He is becoming obstinate and a shade angry also, he glances up at the sun, frowning. Then, as if thinking to himself, he thoughtfully speaks.

"If we carry on it may be into a trouble which I wish to avoid - does not help in gaining control.. If we camp in the village and try to coax their confidence in the morning that will be bad, too. For it will mean keeping them out of their village all night, to be eaten alive by mosquitoes. They would be growing madder hour by hour and probably attack us. No, we'd better go, they will be a little more used to us next visit. So - we can't delay further. We've got to cross that swamp by sundown at the very latest."

And instantly you are as anxious as the guide and crew boys to be away. The P.O. gives a message to the three relieved villagers to be relayed to the Luluai, leaves a few presents as signs of goodwill, and we are out of the stockades. You, although you stroll confidently beside the P.O., are really in as much of a hurry as the crew boys; if not more so. For, after all, they are used to swamps whereas you are not-with sundown coming on.

And the trip back is sheer nightmare.

The morning dawns when you are on the Sepik again. What a safe, cosy home the little pinnace seems as you chug up stream, passing the villages of Asmungua, Japinaut, Nongrumeri, Yumanumbo and Japandei, small places these, probably offshoots of larger villages, or else depleted in tribal fighting. Quite evidently under Government control, these villages are clean and neat, the grass cut, the well-kept gardens lining the river bank, the people showing no sign of timidity. Their House Tarnborans give less attractive evidence of the rapid advance of civilization, for these are "modern" structures, revealing little evidence of any culture of the past. Jerry-builders have also been at work on the dwelling houses; they exhibit neither the thought nor grandeur of the past, a few seasons will see them very dilapidated. Pleased though you are that the headhunting days are vanishing fast, you feel it will be a shame if the wonderful building and extraordinary carving artistry vanishes also.

What a lot you have learnt since, bored for want of something else to pass the time, you set out to explore the Story of the Swamps!

At Japandei village the launch leaves astern the last of the culture and " talk" of the "Middle River," or "Big Sepik"; soon you enter the Upper River at Avatip where your rapidly growing awareness shows you another distinct change in "talk" and culture.

These Avatip natives have been particularly blessed by their mother the river, for with her might, from away back in the mountains, she tears down huge trees and brings to their very doors all the logs they need for their buildings and canoes. Not only does she wrench them out and transport them right to the door, but she holds them there until in their own cheerful time the people take their critical pick before giving her back the refuse-that she may carry it away for them!

A great whirlpool collects, and holds all these logs. You watch it tearing round and round, angry masses of brown waters whirling huge logs and grassy islets in a mad, ceaseless dance. All so silently, not a sound as the big logs spin round in a dizzy chasing of their fellows. For a small present the eager canoe men race out for a big log you fancy. Taught the secret by their fathers from infancy, they seize their chance, dart in, and with what appears a marvellous dexterity pole that great log out from the raging waters and quietly guide it to the bank.

Logs not wanted are poled out from the whirlpool and away they shoot downstream.

You are a civilized man and you know and do things. But you would give a very great deal to possess the nerve, the skill and knowledge, the joyous agility of these brown-skinned masters of the maelstrom.

32

THE FARTHEST OUTPOST

CHUGGING upstream from Avatip, and a welcome sight breaks the monotony of the last two hundred miles of grass, the foothills of the Hunstein Range. And then comes Malu village, nestling beneath a long, densely wooded mountain ridge that rises steeply from the water's edge. You cannot keep your eyes from those massive, sombre green mountains whose summits away ahead vanish up into floating clouds. Yes, you are nearing the mountains at last and yet the big, silent river is still a quarter of a mile wide. The crew boys are cheery, all eager smiles, for to them here comes journey's end. Just round the next bend past Malu, and they laugh and point towards Ambunti, now but two miles farther ahead, while you gaze with interested curiosity, for this is the white man's farthest outpost. And this last fortnight you have been learning what such things mean. Here is the limit, the present limit, set on the farthest boundary line of wildest savagery. Behind you, the controlled river. Beyond Ambunti a maze of great mountain ranges peopled by unknown scores of thousands of wild men, quite unknowing the white man, and unknown to the white man. Some with cultures of their own, others simply "chauash", wild human beings governed by mysterious cults and fears and blood lusts, living sorcery-haunted lives, living in a world of their own, believing they are the world. What strange things, what strange sights lie deep within the as yet impenetrable mystery of those mighty mountains! You wonder and wonder as Ambunti draws rapidly nearer.

The Patrol Officer nods ahead and explains that but two years before the government vessel *Elevala*, with fine seamanship, steamed one hundred and twelve miles farther up river to wait for Karius and Champion, the D.O. aboard to help and welcome them should they succeed. By the tone of voice as he says "Karius and Champion" you detect the awed admiration reflected in his face.

You have never even heard of Karius and Champion. Yet, with the most scanty resources, with a handful of native police and but fifty-nine carriers, they crossed New Guinea. That is, from six hundred miles up the Fly River in Papua, over the great Victor Emanuel Ranges, then down into the valley of the Sepik. Most of those ranges are a frightful country of broken limestone, fantastic as a nightmare of Dante. You have been a short trip up the Fly with me, you've travelled hundreds of miles along the Sepik with your friend the Patrol Officer, but you've no idea of the majesty, the might, the terror of that vast mass of ranges that is the backbone of New Guinea, separating Dutch New Guinea from ours. You know quite a lot of the many attempts before our explorers succeeded in crossing our own Blue Mountains. Well, the Blue Mountains are solid, blessed with long periods of perfect weather, and only three thousand feet high. Where Karius and Champion climbed on foot to cross the Victor Emanuel the gap they at last found was at nine thousand feet, while the Tabletop extended higher to twelve thousand feet. Then again, it is a country of torrential rain every day, of dense jungle, alternating with a weird moss world of bitter cold. Walking cat-like over soggy moss, feet and yards deep, but in places so treacherously fragile that a man could slip straight through and go crashing down into a subterranean ravine, crawling along day after day hungry, wet, miserable, racked with malaria, liable to be attacked at any moment by mountain tribes that had never seen a white man, held up by countless mountain torrents, by impassable swamps. Imagine with what delight then the starving, fever-stricken wretches finally found a gap, crawled on, and at last gazed far over and down into the magnificent valley of the Sepik!

That little handful carried out the biggest exploration job of any attempted in New Guinea by Dutch, German, or Australian. And, believe me, that is saying something.

Yet apart from the New Guinea folk but very few people indeed have ever heard of Karius and Champion. We do not give enough publicity to those who truly deserve it. You realize this as you listen to the experienced Patrol Officer, a man who knows, telling you of this truly remarkable exploit.

The outpost now lies plainly cradled down where the river makes a horseshoe bend towards the mountains. A number of well laid out little buildings. Increased awareness of native life now directs your sight instinctively towards the House Kiap, perched well up on a long spur that descends to the water's edge. A large, barn-shaped building this, guyed down with ropes and kunda vines against storms. Lower down the ridge is the Patrol Officer's house, below which is the "House Paper" (office), the store, with the Medical Assistant's quarters close by the Native Hospital and dispensary. To the west, stand the Native Police Barracks, then the labourers' quarters and married quarters built upon a flat adjacent to the parade ground. Then, farther back towards the deep line of bush, the jail down below the House Kiap. All strongly, well built of native materials, all neat and tidy. The nearby ridges have been cleared of timber and are now bright green under banana-trees. A sac-sac swamp had been cleared of palms and debris and now is a luxuriant Station garden growing rows of maize, sugarcane, pineapples, yams, and watermelons.

Native prisoners, in their pink-striped lap-laps are drilling under instruction by native warders. Others are excavating the site for a new building. Many labourers are carrying out routine work and improvements, others working in the gardens. Musically, laughter comes floating from the ridge down across the water. Quite an imposing little outpost. And it gives you a big thrill to see, lazily flying from the tall flagpole, your own Australian flag.

Once again you are reminded of similar scenes described in books written about big nations taming native countries, which you have read never dreaming that your own nation for long past has been doing the very same thing. And in actually untamed country, among unknown hundreds of thousands of virile, fighting savages and headhunters. But doing it quietly, peacefully, and without exploitation, let alone slavery. Somehow, you cannot help thinking all the better of your country.

At this present time, in this particular area far isolated from the coast, among these scores of thousands of wild people, some four white men are stationed here. Their job is to control and patrol thousands of square miles of swamps, lakes, vast grass areas, towering, heavily timbered mountains and their torrential streams, and dense jungle country wherein live a great population of savages whose tribal wars, raids, and head-hunting expeditions must be kept constantly in check.

The D.O. in spotless whites comes down to the landing to greet your friend the P.O. The D.O. is all alone, for Mr R. S. Pickwell, the Medical Assistant, is away down river conducting a medical patrol, while the Station P.O. has gone to distant Rabaul as escort to twenty-eight headhunters committed for sentence to the Central Court, Rabaul, over a thousand miles away.

So you find yourself politely ensconced in the House Kiap at Ambunti, with a strong feeling that you are going to travel no farther This Headquarters was established but four years before your arrival.
Captain Woodward, on loan from the Papuan Service, was the first District Officer. A very brave woman helped him, his wife. Imagine for a moment her life out there, nearly five hundred miles from the nearest white woman.

Since then, officials Appleby, Feldt, Calcutt and Townsend, preceding your present D.O., Colonel Woodman, have carried on the fast-developing work 235 miles from the river mouth, steadily bringing the natives under control and consolidating the Government's influence.

But you have no part in carrying the white man's burden, you are merely a stray traveller having a "look-see" at swamps. Within a few days you tentatively suggest that you'd like a trip on into those mountains.

Quite nicely the D.O. explains the difficulties - and anyway there are no interpreters, which of course means it would be useless to venture farther.

And of course you've got enough sense to know this is the official, the polite way of saying, "Thus far but no farther."

Anyway, you have seen swamps and swamp life such as you never dreamed existed. And in doing so you have also learned of a great work your country is and has been doing for long past. And you feel the better for the knowing.

As you sail down the silent brown river on the return trip you almost feel you are one with it, you have seen, have felt just a glimpse of its might and mystery, it has taught you such a very great amount.

And you are a better man for the knowing.

Native carvings from the Middle and Upper Sepik in the unique
collection of Colonel H.E. Woodman, D.S.O.
Inset: A natibve house on the Sepik River, New Guinea.

ETT IMPRINT has the following ION IDRIESS books in print in 2024:

Prospecting for Gold (1931)
Lasseter's Last Ride (1931)
Flynn of the Inland (1932)
The Desert Column (1932)
Men of the Jungle (1932)
Drums of Mer (1933)
Gold-Dust and Ashes (1933)
The Yellow Joss (1934)
Man Tracks (1935)
Over the Range (1937)
Forty Fathoms Deep (1937)
Madman's Island (1938)
Headhunters of the Coral Sea (1940)
Lightning Ridge (1940)
Nemarluk (1941)
Shoot to Kill (1942)
Sniping (1942)
Guerrilla Tactics (1942)
Trapping the Jap (1942)
Lurking Death (1942)
The Scout (1943)
Horrie the Wog Dog (1945)
In Crocodile Land (1946)
The Opium Smugglers (1948)
The Wild White Man of Badu (1950)
Outlaws of the Leopolds (1952)
The Red Chief (1953)
The Silver City (1956)
Coral Sea Calling (1957)
Back O' Cairns (1958)
The Wild North (1960)
Tracks of Destiny (1961)
Gouger of the Bulletin (2013)
Ion Idriess: The Last Interview (2020)
Ion Idriess Letters (2023)
Walkabout (2024)